A Stranger in the Village

Sara Alexi is the author of the Greek Village Series. She divides her time between England and a small village in Greece.

http://www.saraalexi.com
http://facebook.com/authorsaraalexi

Sara Alexi

A SELF EFFACING MAN

oneiro

Published by Oneiro Press 2016

Copyright © Sara Alexi 2016

This book is a work of fiction. Names, characters, businesses, organisations, places and events are either the product of the author's imagination or are used fictitiously. Any resemblance to actual persons, living or dead, events or locales is entirely coincidental

ISBN-13:
978-1539379447

ISBN-10:
1539379442

Chapter 1

It is her and yet it is not her. Her hands clutch a single white lily, her hair is woven with petals, her white blouse can hardly be seen for blossoms and in such a setting she should look beautiful.

Cosmo fixes his gaze on her mouth. He has never seen it closed for so long, her tongue so still. Such a terrible silence, her lips sewn together. His chest lifts as he draws in enough air to ease the stinging behind his eyes.

'*Silipitiria*' Mitsos leans over Cosmo's shoulder and whispers his condolences.

It does not feel real to Cosmo, more like a performance in a television drama, and he has the sensation of being outside himself, hovering above the scene, looking down on another Cosmo. The scene before him swims in unspilt tears and he has to make an effort to focus again, to bring back the harsh edges of reality. Then it is all a blur once more, and he forces his thoughts, his emotions, back under his command until his tears are stifled again.

'*Zoi se esena.*' Stella, Mitsos's wife, adds her own sympathies, and the two quietly step up to the waxen-faced woman lying in his mama's place and cross themselves three times, finishing with a thumbnail to the lips before shuffling away to the front row of wooden chairs in the gloom. Vasso, who runs the kiosk in the square, is already seated and she acknowledges Mitsos and Stella with a nod. She was the first to arrive to pay her respects to the woman she knew as Florentia. Behind Vasso is Marina, who runs the corner shop in the square, crossing herself earnestly when the priest's cantations reach certain points. She is with her son, Petta, and his wife, Irini. Beside them is Theo. It is strange to see Theo out of the *kafenio* where he makes coffee all day long at the top of the square, a commanding place for anyone to sit – as long as he is male. Theo crosses himself too, but hesitantly, and not at the same time as Marina. He is not a regular churchgoer.

The church is so full it could be the Easter service, but instead of happy faces there are slack cheek muscles, downward-curling mouths and watering eyes. Cosmo gazes, almost unseeing, over the sea of faces he has known all his life.

Alongside the people he sees every day are some who are slightly less well known to him: Kyria Sophia, who lives next to Marina and sometimes used to help out in the shop before Marina's son and wife moved in with her, is here, and so is Sakis the musician, who has taken a seat next to her. On the end of the row, by himself, is Babis the lawyer – the 'lawyer for the people' – as he likes to be known. Cosmo cannot help but wonder why he is here: neither he nor his mama knew him. On the next row is the very familiar sight of Poppy, who sells everything and anything out of her tiny one-room emporium opposite the back of their house. *His* house now, he corrects himself. He bites his lip.

He looks again at the woman who is his mama, who is not his mama. Her skin looks like it is made from church candles – not the brown beeswax ones, but the transparent white ones – and she appears to be sweating, not in droplets through her pores, but with an all-over sheen. To the mouth that will never open again the undertakers have applied lipstick. When did she ever wear lipstick? A snort of mirth escapes him before he can control himself.

With a squeeze of his shoulder, Thanasis returns to his seat next to Cosmo. The church warden has put out six chairs, three either side of the coffin, which is end on to the ornate *iconostasis* with its renditions of the saints and angels in bright colours, edged in gold. These seats are reserved for family, but there is only Cosmo who can rightfully claim one, and he is relieved that Thanasis has sat next to him, releasing him from his isolation.

'So they went over the top with the flowers anyway,' Thanasis mutters, waving his hand at the columns that are decorated with vast swathes of lilies. 'Have they told you what they are charging yet?'

The *psaltis* drones, his tuneless song rising to the rafters. Cosmo can just see him standing behind a display of flowers. He wears jeans and a T-shirt as if he does not expect to be seen. His mouth moves and the plaintive call is dramatically echoed around the small church, but his face is vacant.

The priest, centre stage, answers with his own lament. His hair is neatly tied back, his beard combed and his cassock covered with a gold-edged white habit that drops to his waist. His eyes drift around the church, unfocused; his lips move but the sounds coming out of them seem disconnected from him. He looks down, picks at a mark on his tunic, then lifts the fabric to inspect it. Satisfied, he drops the garment, all the while continuing with his monosyllabic wail. An edge of irritation begins to build inside Cosmo, but it snuffs out before it has gained any hold. Theirs is just a job like any other; why should they care?

He is not going to look at her again. It is not her anyway. He shifts in his seat, eager for the ordeal to be over. Thanasis's hand squeezes his shoulder again and Cosmo tries to concentrate, take his mind anywhere except to where it is unwillingly drawn. He has never understood the words of any of the services, although he has been to them all, fifty-five times. Fifty-five Ascensions, fifty-five Pentecosts, and fifty-five of everything else, sitting next to his mama, and last Sunday was his - he painstakingly does the maths, blocking from his mind any other thoughts or emotions for a good two minutes -two thousand, eight hundred and sixtieth Sunday service by her side. But the ecclesiastical Greek of the ceremonies has always been unintelligible to him, and he has sat blankly through every one of the performances he has witnessed ever since he can remember. If it had not been for his mama nudging him to cross himself, to stand, to sit, as she mouthed along with the service as if joining in with a pop song, he would have slept through every one of them. Or not gone at all, given the choice.

He looks at her unmoving face again, an empty shell. She is no longer there, and he has choices now.

The priest is on the move. The censer swings back and forth, releasing incense-permeated smoke that twists and coils up towards the ceiling. A shaft of sunlight from the open doors highlights the plumes as they disperse towards the heavens.

Cosmo breathes in deeply, enjoying the heady scent. He can identify frankincense and myrrh, but also, perhaps, cedar? She burns cedar and myrrh on a Sunday, at home, he thinks to himself, and then corrects himself – burnt, not burns. The priest makes his way down the central aisle of the church, spreading clouds of incense from the censer, which he swings, jangling it on its chain. For Cosmo, the smell is synonymous with a day of rest and one of her good dinners, but today the familiar scent gives him no comfort. He should have brought a handkerchief. He did not expect to experience these waves of emotion, this lifting in his lungs, a tightening across his chest, a panic in his heart, a stinging behind his eyes. His lips tremble and Thanasis shoves a pristine white hanky into his hands, and even though Cosmo feels he might be swamped by these unfamiliar emotions, a part of him calmly wonders why Thanasis has a hanky and where in his little cottage he could possibly keep such an item clean. Thanasis's life is all dusty donkeys and manure.

Then the service is over and the congregation stands as the men from the funeral parlour heave the coffin onto their shoulders. Cosmo is carried along with the throng, out of the church doors and into the hot sunshine where people shake his hand and pat his shoulder and whisper words of kindness and sympathy again and again. Most of the men light up, and there is a low murmur of relieved conversation.

'She could have been carried by one person,' Cosmo tells Thanasis as they watch the men load the coffin in the car. 'She was so thin, never ate.'

'Ah, but she could cook,' Thanasis replies, and a new wave of panic flutters in Cosmo's chest. Who will cook for him now? Who will mend his shirts and keep house? A wife would have softened that blow, but oh no, there was never one good enough for her son. The one or two girls he brought home when he was younger were not made to feel at ease, and now he is too old and she is dead and he is alone. She didn't think of that, did she? She kept him to herself to chide and deride, and to ensure there was someone to look after her in her old age, but now who will look after him?

And what of the orange orchards? She didn't share the running of them with him either, so now that is also a problem.

He follows the car as it starts off towards the cemetery, inching past Marina's shop, a slow right turn into the square.

Take the job of postman, she said. The pension is good, and how hard can it be to deliver a few letters around the village? Huh! What did she know!

'Don't you fuss over how the orchards are run,' she used to say. Well, there is no avoiding that fuss now, is there, because who is there to teach him the ways of the farm in her absence? Who else is there to deal with the workers and organise the harvest and the buyers when that time comes? She didn't ever think how that would be for him, did she!

'Eh, Cosmo, come, we'd better keep up until we get to the cemetery, so there is someone to greet her.' Thanasis takes hold of his elbow and leads him a little faster behind the car.

Stella and Mitsos walk arm in arm by his side, supportive, but clinging to each other. He is older than her by a good few years, and it is Stella who will find herself alone. But she will manage – she can manage anything. Irini holds Petta's hand. Those two are about the same age. Which one of them will be left to face their old age all alone? At least they have a son, and he will never desert them.

Why could he not have had a normal life, Cosmo wonders? Why would she not let him have a normal life? Did she not realise that he would have loved her all the more for it?

'*Ela*, Cosmo, we are here.' Thanasis guides him through the cemetery gates.

Chapter 2

There are two ouzo bottles, but as he reaches towards them they merge into one.

'Thanasi, where d'you go? Thanasi?' Cosmo lifts his head and looks around the kitchen. The washed pots, neatly stacked on the plate rack above the sink, come into focus and recede again. Then a bumpy line above the rack sharpens and straightens, to become the lace-draped shelf of canisters for the sugar, coffee, flour and goodness knows what else. There is the crocheted filigree she made herself many years ago, sitting outside the back door on her wooden kitchen chair, talking to Poppy in the half-light of evening. It was white and fine when his mama first pinned it to the front of that shelf; over the years it has become grey, and now it hangs stiffly, catching the dust. He turns his head to one side. The shelf was always just too high for her to reach without the little stool she kept behind the door. He frowns. Why in all the years since his baba died has he never, until this moment, thought to put up a lower shelf?

'Sorry, Mama,' he mutters, and a series of sobs jerk at his body.

'Thanasi!' he calls again.

The dishcloth by the stained and cracked marble sink is folded into a triangle, as always, just as she left it. He wants to grab it, mess it up, throw it to the floor, but, right now, his weight is too great and his legs will not do his bidding. She always folded it into a triangle. Why?

'Why would you do that?' he asks the ceiling and then adds, over his shoulder, 'Thanasi? Where are you? Did you hear the priest, reciting his meaningless words over her grave? Philomena, he called her. Philomena! He didn't even know her name was Florentia!'

He grabs for the ouzo bottle, which seems to come alive in his grip. It leaves the table and takes his hand upwards, directionless, passing through the air with no clear destination. Then he remembers to bend his elbow and the bottle comes more or less under his control, and the rim approaches his mouth. Lips pursed, he waits. Contact. His teeth jangle with the impact and the clear liquid burns a track down his throat. He sets the bottle down with a thud and wipes his mouth, chin and neck on the back of his hand.

'Thanasi?' he calls again, and he tries to stand.

The table rocks as he steadies himself against it. The kitchen is empty; there is no Thanasis. And then he recalls and waves a finger in front of his face.

'Donkey feeding.' He looks out of the window into the dark of the night. 'So take a seat again, my friend.' He invites himself to sit and turns to reassure himself that the chair is still there. His left foot tucks behind his right, his weight falls forward, his instinct sends out a hand and he grabs the chair, pushing it over with his weight, and he and the chair sprawl on the floor. His sack, which was hung over the back of the chair, falls with him and the letters he collected from the post office in Saros the day before yesterday, in a time when she was still alive, scatter across the floor, skidding across the rough painted surface.

'*Gamoto!*' Cosmo curses and tries to roll over onto all fours, which takes more effort than he expected and he huffs and puffs with the exertion. He puts his hand down for support, but his palm lands on a letter, which slides along the floor under his weight and then suddenly shoots away, taking his hand with it. His ribs take the brunt of the impact, and his chin catches on a chair leg.

'*Gamo tin Panagia ...*' His profanity increases, and he lies still for a moment so his breathing can return to normal. His face has come to rest on a selection of letters, the corner of one of them digging into his cheek. He reaches to remove it and eyes the offending missive.

He eyes widen, his mouth opens.

'Please no!' he gasps. 'No, no, not now.' And tears spring to his eyes, and all the sorrow and sadness he has done so well to hold back since the shock of the old woman's death rushes to discharge itself, merging with a host of new emotions. Lying on his back, the letter clutched to his chest with both hands, his knees contracting upward, he wails at the top of his voice.

'You take one but you cannot take both!' he shouts at the rafters. 'You hear me, God?' Then he rolls onto his side, curls into the foetal position and lets himself cry and cry until, eventually, he falls asleep.

The cold of the dawn wakes him, seeping into his bones from the painted concrete floor. That, and a banging headache. The first thing to come into focus is the cuff of his shirt, which has frayed at the edge and needs to be carefully trimmed and sewn over. He will ask his mama to do that today. He blinks. But why is he wearing his best shirt? He looks around him. And why is he lying on the kitchen floor? His head hammers from the inside.

Images of the lowering coffin suck the breath from his chest but no tears come. In their place is a sense of panic. Who will mend his clothes now, darn his socks, cook his food, keep the house, deal with the logistics of the orange orchards? Who did she hire to do the jobs around the farm?

'Too much,' he says out loud, and he closes his eyes again and curls up as small as he can. He feels the coolness of paper in his hands, which are pressed against his chest. He uncurls enough to see what it is.

The sight of the handwriting brings a new horror, a fresh twist of the knife in his heart.

'No.' The word hisses out like a curse. Grabbing the upturned chair leg and then the edge of the table, he manages to stand, the letter still in his hand. The room spins; he feels sick. He closes his eyes and everything steadies. With the chair set upright again, he sits heavily.

When was the last of these letters? They used to come every six months or so but the last one, when did that come? Two years ago, three, more? And for how long after reading that last letter did the feeling of awkwardness last between him and Maria? Four months? Probably more like six. He would not be able to stand that now, not now his mother is gone. Now it should go the other way; the distance should close.

He turns the letter over. Only the very end of the flap is stuck down and with the slightest flick it would come open. He could read what is written and maybe that would help him to deal with it. But is there even a need to look? There will be the faded, lined paper, torn from a school notebook, yellowed with age, and with a stain in the top left-hand corner, just like all the others since the first of these letters, over twenty years ago now. The content, the words themselves, will just be a variation of all the others and no good will come of it.

He looks at her name, in all-too-familiar writing on the front, her address below. Whatever is written will do her no good and will only cause her pain.

He could burn it! Just make it disappear. But that would be dishonest. He is the postman, his job is to deliver the post, this one just like all the rest. What if it says something different from the others written by the same hand?

He turns it over again. He could open it – just take a little look, not read it all through. Just get the tone. If it is the same, then he could burn it and save himself and her the angst.

His fingers hover over the point, his nail against its edge. Just a flick of his finger would do it.

'No.' Cosmo defiantly puts the envelope down on the table and snatches his hands away as if the very paper has scalded him, each hand tucked under the opposite armpit. 'You are the postman, you deliver letters, that is your job.'

He looks at the letter hard, her name scrawled like spiders' legs.

'This is so unfair. Why now?' he wails to no one.

He picks the envelope up again and turns it over. It is hardly sealed at all.

Chapter 3

The next morning, leaving his coffee half drunk on the kitchen table, Cosmo repacks his satchel, gathering up the letters from where they are still scattered across the floor. He will do his rounds; delivering the mail is an important responsibility and must be done, despite his heaviness of limb and heart and the throbbing in his head. Did his mama not go to talk to the orange buyers the day after his baba's funeral? Did she not go herself and water the trees on the very evening of the day he died?

He lifts the bag over his head and slings it across his back.

The new day is full of the freshness of spring, and it helps to soothe the thickness in his head. The light breeze is warm but not hot, and there are one or two light, fluffy white clouds in the sky that the sun might hide behind so, before closing the door, Cosmo reaches and grabs his grey, shapeless cotton jacket, the one with the hole in the left pocket from the hook where his coats hang with his mama's. Even on a warm day, the breeze from the bike can be cooling.

'Good morning, Cosmo. Surely you are not going to deliver the post today?' Poppy is sitting in the doorway of her emporium opposite, sipping coffee from a tiny cup. The window display looks different. The brightly coloured beach balls that were there yesterday have been moved and the mannequin that usually displays a multicoloured crocheted tank top over a vivid shirt is wearing a black jacket over the top, and a poorly painted icon is resting against her pale plastic leg. Poppy was fond of his mama, and they drank coffee together every day in the kitchen, with his mama slicing vegetables for whatever she was going to cook that day and Poppy pricing new items for the shop – or repricing old ones that still bore their price in drachmas. Often a plate of food would go over to Poppy's, and more than once Cosmo has rescued one of his mama's plates from being displayed for sale in Poppy's window. Often, too, Poppy would come over to the house to eat, staying to keep Mama company when he wandered up to the square for a coffee at Theo's.

'It is too soon for you to go back to work, Cosmo,' Poppy tells him. 'Come, let's have a coffee together.' She takes hold of the arms of her white plastic chair and leans forward, readying herself to stand.

'The mail must be delivered.' Cosmo is emphatic.

'But surely not today?' Poppy relaxes her grip on the chair, her weight sinking into her ballooning black skirts. There is disappointment in her voice and her eyebrows are raised.

'I have already missed two days,' Cosmo mumbles as he climbs onto his little bike. He might have to take something for his headache. A decorative glass evil eye hangs from the keys in the bike's ignition. After losing them once, years ago, he now leaves them permanently in the ignition and he has never lost them since. With a twist, the motor starts and he pulls away without another word.

As Cosmo leaves the village, heading for Saros where he will pick up the mail, he does not see Thanasis sauntering into the *kafenio*.

Yesterday's cigarette smoke still lingers in the air but the smell of freshly brewed coffee dominates the masculine domain. From across the square, with the breeze in this direction, the aroma of freshly made bread mixes with them both in the early-morning air. Thanasis yawns and for a moment all scents are lost to him. He did not sleep well last night. Someone left a donkey tied to his gate last night, abandoned. It is not the first time. Nor is he a fool. He knows people do not give away animals for nothing, but he hoped at first it was just a case of someone not needing her, rather than not being able to afford to keep her. But now he suspects laminitis. A ridge of fat where her mane springs from is a symptom that this diagnosis could fit.

He yawns again; he is not in the best of moods. Just the prospect of caring for an animal with laminitis is exhausting. The poor creature's food will have to be carefully monitored – Thanasis will have to limit her foraging. At this time of year this means keeping her in the stable, alone; she will not be able to go out with the others. The poor animal will bray out her loneliness. Thanasis blinks hard; he will be around to give her company. If he creates an enclosure near the pump, at least he can make sure she has plenty to drink.

'There he goes,' Grigoris remarks. 'Off for his first coffee in Saros.' This is followed by a snigger and a slurp of his own coffee. Thanasis follows Grigoris's gaze to see who he is talking about. Cosmo is driving slowly out of the square.

'He's going for the mail,' Thanasis responds, and he sits at a table by the nicotine-yellow wall, alone. He rubs at his eyes. Maybe he will just have to put the animal down; it depends how bad it is, how well she responds. The corners of his mouth turn down.

'Ach, you are too kind to him, but his nature is well known,' replies Vasillis, who is sitting with Grigoris. It pulls Thanasis back from his grim thoughts. He does not look at the others, his eyes remain downcast. The floor is still wet in places where Theo has mopped it, and a cloth and a bottle of glass cleaner are by the metal-rimmed glass door set in the floor-to-ceiling windows at the front.

'The man has never done a full day's work in his life,' Grigoris continues, in defence of his remark. 'He will get a shock now his mama is gone and there is no one to cook and wait on him.'

He picks up the soft packet of cigarettes on the table and taps one out with a flick; it flips over in the air and he catches it in his mouth as if he has done this a thousand times before, which he has. He leans his head sideways as he sparks his lighter.

'A bit of respect, boys.' Theo comes to Thanasis's table to take his order, but Thanasis is not sure he wants to stay. He might go back and take another look at the animal's hoofs now it is light and he is more awake.

He looks out across the square after his friend. He must make time for Cosmo now too. No matter how the man got on with his mama, her dying so suddenly like that is a massive shock and will prompt huge changes. Poor Cosmo's world is going to be a little unsettled for a while. A bit of kindness is what he will need, not this unfriendly slander. He picks up his keys.

'Actually, Theo–' he begins.

'Pay them no mind,' Theo says quietly, a hand on his shoulder keeping him seated. 'Frappe?' he asks, and Thanasis resettles himself with a nod.

Spiros lumbers in. His shirt is too short for his long body, his boots clattering on the steps as if he has trouble controlling his feet. *'Kalimera,'* he says to everyone.

'Another man who never works?' Grigoris says, but this time with a smile. Spiros looks around and behind him to see which company he is in and spots the distant figure of Cosmo leaving the village.

'I suggest you keep your comments to yourself,' Thanasis barks.

'What?' Grigoris sounds as if he has been caught off guard.

'You heard me.' Thanasis growls.

'Come on, man, it's not like it's a secret!' He smirks now, encouraging Spiros and Vasillis to join in. 'He wanders into town at his leisure, picks up the mail in his own good time, goes home, sorts the mail on his kitchen table with a coffee to hand – we have all seen him.'

He looks at Vasillis and Spiros, who are now both sitting at his table, and they both half-heartedly agree, with sideways nods and raised eyebrows.

'Then he meanders about on that little bike of his, his head in the air, looking over gates and walls, so he does not miss a thing that is happening in the village, and he calls this his delivery service. I tell you, he spends more time talking than posting. Some mail comes days late.

You know this and I know this,' Grigoris counters.

'Keep your mouth shut,' Thanasis growls.

'Or what?' Grigoris puts his cigarette in the ashtray. Vasillis rests a hand on his neighbour's arm and makes a tutting noise.

'You swill your bad thoughts around in public as if you have a right! You don't know Cosmo's life – you see what you see and you make the rest up. If we did that with your life, you would fare no better. So shut up and stay quiet.' He can feel the calluses on his palms as he balls his fingers into a fist.

He hadn't meant to speak out like that, and he is not sure whether to stand and make trouble or grab his keys and leave.

Theo walks between his table and Grigoris's, creating a wall with his own body in a pretence of serving Thanasis his frappe.

'I might have put too much sugar in that. Take a sip while I'm here. If it is too sweet I'll make another.' And Theo remains standing so that Thanasis cannot see Grigoris, nor Grigoris Thanasis.

Thanasis is too angry to sip the drink; he cannot even uncurl his fingers.

'It's fine,' he barks, the permanent lines between his brows deeply indented.

'Well, just to be sure, I will let you check,' Theo says calmly, making it clear that he is not moving before Thanasis tastes the coffee.

It is half in his mind to leave, but his respect for Theo keeps him in his chair, and after a few seconds he tries his coffee and says it is fine, before Theo returns to his counter.

Cosmo is of course nowhere in sight now. Halfway to Saros and unaware of the bad feeling in the air of the *kafenio*. How many times has Thanasis heard Cosmo's mama call her son lazy, accuse him of incompetence? Didn't he himself absorb this as if it was the truth until, time and time again, he found Cosmo offering to help him with things – with the building of the small stable, and then the wall that got kicked down – and didn't he just grab a shovel and start digging a channel when the road flooded and it all ran into Thanasis's orchard? So many different favours over the years, and all offered willingly. Over time, this caused Thanasis to revise his view of Cosmo. The man is far from lazy. Hampered, perhaps, by his overbearing mama – Thanasis crosses himself three times – but not lazy, and he objects to the likes of Grigoris perpetuating these rumours.

The frappe is good and strong, and the adrenaline that was coursing through his limbs from his stand-off with Grigoris is now replaced with caffeine and he begins to think about his day. He has some corrugated sheeting down at the far end of his small orange grove; he will use that, up against the trunk of the fig tree in the corner of the present enclosure, to create a place for his new donkey. Then she can see the others outside without grazing herself. He need only keep her in for the next month or so; then the greenery will have all dried out and she can roam with no danger of overeating.

Cosmo appreciates the normality of the gentle, slow puttering on his bike. Should he deliver the letters he has in his satchel now and then go for the new mail in the sorting office in Saros town, or collect the new mail first and deliver them all at the same time? He drives towards the road that leads out of the village, passing whitewashed cottages with terracotta roof tiles, and doorsteps that are guarded on either side by painted olive oil tins or unglazed ceramic pots bursting with bright geraniums. The houses that are set back from the road's edge have arches of flowers over the gates. He remembers when it became a fashion, years ago, back when he was a teenager, and the women planted bougainvillea and wild roses to create their displays, and these have continued to grow and blossom ever since. They are all in flower right now, and it somehow feels wrong that life is blossoming so defiantly when his mama lies in an as-yet-unmarked grave.

He turns his thoughts back to his work. It would be a heavy bag if he were to collect any new mail from Saros. Also, if he goes to the depot he will see the postmaster, and the others in the sorting room, and then there will be the women who work on the counters as well. They will all want to extend their sympathies, fuss over his loss, make him remember, think of it, of her waxen face, all over again.

From the moment he was told of her death he wanted to remember nothing. But it is from that moment that his life has seemed to be a loop being replayed over and over again in his head.

Chapter 4

It was a normal fishing excursion, just like any other. He'd eaten the bread and feta, and drunk his wine too, and the boat had rocked gently to the rhythm of the waves, like any other day. He had not caught a single fish, as usual. On his return, it was a little odd to see not just Petros, who liked to hang about the harbour, but also Petros's mama Niki waiting for him as he shipped the oars and let the boat slip silently up to the jetty.

'Cosmo, they say you must go to the hospital,' Niki said nervously, her gaze forced: the fake calm of panic. Cosmo waited to hear no more. Something in her tone made him leap on his bike; the wheels spun as he revved away, Niki shouting something behind him, waving her hands – but he couldn't stop. He had never driven that fast before, and he did not slow down at the roundabout or pause at the junctions. He left his bike blocking the hospital entrance, engine still racing, as he ran inside, demanding the woman behind the glass window tell him where his mama was.

'Name?' she asked, bored, in no hurry, then tapped at the computer, scanning a list as Cosmo shifted from foot to foot.

'When did she come in?' the woman asked, trailing the end of her pen down the rows of admissions.

'Today,' he snapped, and she looked up at him, over her glasses.

'No, no one of that name admitted today.' And at those words, his panic subsided and he wondered if he had jumped to the wrong conclusion when Niki said he must go to the hospital. But why else would she have said such a thing?

Turning from the woman, he came face to face with Doctor Petsokoftis, a man who had attended to his mama when she had spent a week in the hospital some years back with a virus and could not keep her food down.

'*Silipitiria*,' the doctor said kindly – my condolences, and Cosmo's blood ran cold.

The shock must have shown on Cosmo's face because it brought the doctor up short. 'Ah,' he said. 'You have not been told.'

'Yes, they told me to come to the hospital ...' But his blood was no warmer and the hairs on the back of his neck rose up.

'Ah, Cosmo,' the doctor breathed wearily, and the tall man's shoulders drooped and Cosmo knew for sure.

'She had a good long life, and best to go quickly, don't you think?' The doctor spoke quietly, a hand gently holding Cosmo's shoulder.

The room where they had laid her out was cold, and there she was, lying on a stainless steel table in the middle. She still looked like his mama then, her posture relaxed, her mouth slightly open, but with a milky sheen to her eyes, which stared at the ceiling unseeing. He touched her hair, stroked it in a way he would never have done when she was alive. The hospital porter retreated silently and Cosmo bent over her and laid his head on her chest and held her hand. There were no tears at that stage.

He shakes his head. He does not want the sympathies of his work colleagues, not yet, so he pulls up by the school.

The multicoloured railings that surround the school mark the start of the village, if you are approaching from Saros town, and they promised such excitement as a boy: a whole day with other children, and break times in the yard with no parents to remind him of chores that he had not done, or the messes he had made. There are children inside now and the windows are open. Their laughter carries across the hopscotch-painted playground. Complementing their light soprano trills is the deeper voice of the teacher, who is trying, and failing, to contain their energy. To Cosmo it seems just moments since he was in there himself. How Maria had laughed back then, the sun in her hair and her teeth so even and white.

He turns his bike around and takes out the first bunch of letters. Three are for Sakis the musician. There are always quite a few for him. Cosmo is never sure whether Sakis said for him to stack them up when he is away giving concerts, or to keep posting them through his door, and he is embarrassed to ask again. In the village it does not take long for the mice to make themselves at home when people are away: letters make a good a meal and can be shredded for bedding. But Sakis is here now – he was at the funeral – so, either way, these he can post.

The sound of an acoustic guitar filters through the orchard at the back of Sakis's house. It is a sad tune and Cosmo does not want to hear it. He posts the letters and lets the letterbox clang shut. The sound rings through the house, echoing off the ceiling, and the song stops abruptly, replaced by footsteps.

Cosmo picks more letters from his satchel. There is one for old Anna who lives opposite Sakis. It bears a Canadian stamp and will be from her daughter, or perhaps her granddaughter, judging by the childish writing. Cosmo knows what joy it will bring Anna, and he smiles.

She is not fast on her feet any more, and he waits for her to answer his knock. Not that she was ever quick, but she has definitely slowed down in the last year or two. If he was a betting man, which he isn't, he would have laid odds that she would pass before his mama. His bottom lip trembles, and it annoys him, and makes him think of the letter, the one he should deliver but instead has left at home on the kitchen table.

'Ah, Cosmo, I did not expect you today. Come in, do come in. I will make some mountain tea, or would you prefer coffee?'

'Neither, thank you, Kyria Anna.' He accepted once and she kept him there until his stomach had rumbled, and then she insisted on making him food and that had made him sleepy. So then she made up the daybed, which he had no intention of using, but somehow he fell asleep on it half sitting up, and the day disappeared and the day's letters were not delivered. He holds out the envelope.

'Oh, you are a kind boy.'

It amuses him every time she calls him that. She takes the letter, tears it open bit by bit with a crooked finger and pulls out a single sheet, passing it to Cosmo.

'Would you, dear?' she says, and sits at the kitchen table, inviting him to do the same.

'My dearest Grandma Anna,' he begins.

The letter describes how Anna's granddaughter took a dried pomegranate in to show-and-tell. The fruit had come from Anna's tree, last summer when the family visited the village. When he reaches the end, as usual Anna asks him to read it through once more, with moisture glistening in the corners of her eyes.

'Such a sweet child,' she concludes, leaning back in her chair so she can open the drawer beneath the table. She takes out a sheet of paper and a pen and slides them across to Cosmo.

Reading and writing were not Cosmo's strong points at school, but in the twenty-five – no, nearly thirty years he has been the village postman he has had plenty of opportunity to practise both. When he took the job it didn't occur to him that many of his neighbours were even less literate than he was. Many of the older generation are unable to read or write at all, and there are several of his contemporaries who were pulled out of school for one reason or another – generally to help on the family farm – and who never mastered reading and writing.

He flattens the sheet of paper against the tabletop with the edge of his fist and licks the tip of the pencil.

'Right, so – Dear ...'

'Dearest,' Anna corrects him. He writes what she dictates. Occasionally he rephrases something so it reads better, but he makes sure not to embellish or change the essence of what Anna is saying. He tried that once, for an old lady who lived over near Thanasis. She has passed on now, but at the time she was so missing her son in Thessaloniki, who seemed to have very little interest in her. She had Cosmo write about her cough that wouldn't go away, and he exaggerated and made it sound worse than it was, to make the boy more concerned. Well, he was more concerned all right. He was on the next bus down, and lost his job over it, and Cosmo has been very careful ever since.

'You want me to put some crosses for kisses?' he asks.

'No, let me.' Kyria Anna takes the pencil and clumsily adds a cross at the end.

The whole exchange must have taken three quarters of an hour and when he returns to his bike he discovers old Vangelis has a letter, as does Grigoris. That will be another half hour. But for some of the older generation, especially the widows and widowers on the outskirts of the village, these moments, being read the words of their loved ones, is the highlight of their week. It reminds them that they are not alone, that they are loved and considered, and Cosmo never rushes.

People in the village think he is lazy. He knows they do. They have come to that conclusion because he doesn't always get all the letters delivered in a day. He could challenge this view they have of him, but that would mean breaking confidences and he is not about to do that for the sake of a little vanity. Sometimes a letter holds some emotional content, and the recipient needs comforting, or calming, and it is exhausting. If he has had such a morning and he goes home for a coffee, to revive himself so he can continue his work, another villager might see this as shirking, and he has been classed by some as a man with no pride in his work. But what can he say? Should he betray who can read and who cannot – explain that the two hours at Georgia's house was to read her a letter that announced her pension was going to be reduced as part of the austerity measures? Was it not crippling enough for her to hear that the few hundred euros a month she had to feed and clothe herself, keep herself warm in winter and cool in summer, was going to be reduced, without the humiliation of the whole village knowing she was illiterate?

'My last water bill was that amount alone,' she said, and he sat and comforted her, and then, together, they worked out a budget that meant she could survive. He could explain to the postmaster what had held him up, relate in detail how he had spent the morning; however, the postmaster is not naturally discreet – in fact, he is like an old woman in his love of gossip. How long would it be before everyone in the village knew all that had been said if he were the postman! Cosmo shakes his head at the thought. Better to let them think him lazy and inefficient than to embarrass those who cannot read, or those who are in distress. They have their pride just like anyone else.

Neither Vangelis nor Grigoris is in so he puts their letters back in his sack – he'll try again tomorrow – and continues his round. Occasionally he thinks of his mama, but more often he thinks of the letter on the kitchen table at home. He has still not decided if he will deliver it or not.

His route takes him past his mama's orange orchard.

'My orchard.' Even speaking the words aloud do not make it feel real. They will always be hers, her dowry, her mama's before her. How soon before he needs to do something with them? When do they need spraying with chemicals, for example – isn't that in the spring, to make them fatten? He has no idea. Have the weeds been cleared from under the trees, so they do not suck up the water? Is the watering system even turned on?

'Oh, Mama.' He both calls on her and curses her. He needs a coffee. Normally she would make it, and they would sit together and talk. Often, when he had drunk his coffee, she would give him a list of things she wanted from the shops in Saros. That was another reason why he didn't always get all the letters delivered. She never wanted everything from just one shop in Saros. No, he must go to one place for the pasta, and to another for the toilet rolls. She had fixed ideas about which shop was cheapest for which item. As the shops closed at two for *mesimeri*, his workday was often eaten into by this task. In all the time she was alive, he never questioned whether it was reasonable of her to ask this of him. He does now.

'Helping her to save those few cents could have lost me my job,' he says to himself as he drives into the square. There is no point in going home. He does not have the patience it takes to make a good coffee and he can have one at Theo's instead.

The *kafenio* is situated along the top of the square, on the corner, with tall windows on two sides, facing the village shop on one side, and on the other the square and the road that brings visitors from Saros, family from Athens, hawkers, dealers, gypsies collecting scrap, and primary children returning from school. It is the perfect vantage point from which to see all the comings and goings in the village.

Cosmo kicks the stand out on his bike next to a dozen others outside the kafenio. He recognises most of the other bikes and he knows who will be in the *kafenio* before he enters.

Three steps take him into the large, unadorned room with its high ceilings. The walls are bare and the wooden chairs have raffia seats and are time worn, the paint rubbing thin on the top rails and stretchers. There are four seats to each of a dozen or so square wooden tables, the tops of which are sheeted with metal, stark and uncompromising. The pot-bellied stove in the back right-hand corner was the focal point last month, but now, with the spring's heat, the men have spread themselves around the room and the stove is abandoned for the rest of the year. There are no embellishments here, nothing to soften the practicality of the place. It is designed to set a farmer or a postman at his ease. There is nothing a man needs to take care of or treat gently.

'*Yeia sou*, Cosmo,' Theo greets him, and, leaving his low counter to welcome him, he gives him a gentle slap on the back in acknowledgement of his so-recent loss.

'*Ela*.' Thanasis kicks out a chair where he is sitting with Mitsos.

'Coffee?' Theo asks.

'Thanks.' Cosmo slumps heavily into his seat and they sit in silence. In the square the central palm tree casts a spiky shade. Two people are at the kiosk and their voices carry: two farmers sharing a joke with Vasso, who works inside.

'They may as well just change the date on these newspapers and reprint them, for all the actual news they carry,' one is saying.

'Be glad there is no news. It's all horror and shock these days anyway,' the other replies.

'I'll be charging you both for each page you read. Are you going to buy the thing or not?' Vasso is teasing them, on the edge of laughter.

'Ach!' Theo is a naturally quiet man and the exclamation is loud enough to divert the attention of every man in the *kafenio* away from the action in the square.

'Would you look at that!' He holds up his *briki*, the handle in one hand, the tiny pan in the other.

'Ach,' he says again, and he tries to match the two, as if simply doing so will join them again.

'Don't you have another?' Mitsos asks. 'Do you want me to go and get you one from the eatery?' He raises a finger, vaguely pointing past the kiosk to the *ouzeri* he runs with Stella.

'Nah, I have another ... But – well, you know how it is, you get used to the feel of the thing, the weight, the balance.'

'Best not to get attached to these things,' says a man leaning on his shepherd's crook by the cold stove.

'Ah, but you do, don't you,' Mitsos replies, and several of the men nod.

'I still have an old pencil I got when I was at school,' the shepherd says.

'And what would you want with a pencil?' Thanasis laughs.

'Cleans his ears with it,' a farmer with his sleeves rolled up and a bushy moustache retorts.

Mitsos chuckles and Theo throws the *briki* in the bin with a clang of metal against metal. The banter continues. Someone has a ruler that was bought for him when he went to school and now he has passed it on to his grandchild, and someone else has a *skeparni* that he remembers his baba buying when he was only twelve, and they continue to list the things they have stored, or used, for decades. Theo makes coffee in the new *briki*, tutting and sighing as he does so. After pouring the contents into a little cup, he puts it in front of Cosmo and looks at it, shaking his head.

Cosmo drinks the brew and feels somewhat revived and, leaving his bike, walks home almost with a bounce to his step. It is only when his hand is on the door and his lips are poised to announce to his mama that he is home that he sniffs the air, smells no food cooking and remembers that now he is entirely alone.

On the kitchen table, instead of plates and cutlery laid out for two, there is only the letter next to the box of matches. He had forgotten about that too.

Chapter 5

Cosmo picks up the letter and turns it over. A part of him clings to the vain hope that he was so drunk last night that he was mistaken – that he had a paranoid delusion. But there can be no mistaking the handwriting, and if he opens the envelope, he knows, the message inside will be written on lined paper, torn down one side as if from a school exercise book, and it will have a stain in the top left-hand corner where at some point the book got wet. He replaces the envelope back on the table and takes a deep breath, then lets it out noisily. Who is he to play God? There is nothing for it: he must deliver it, and accept all it brings.

He looks around the kitchen blankly. He never liked the pale-green that his mama insisted he apply every five years or so to the walls and the home-made cupboard doors, to freshen them up. Maybe he will change it now. White, perhaps, to make the room feel airy, light.

Right now, though, he needs food, and this is a challenge. Pans! There were often pans on the stove and dishes in the oven. Where did she keep them? He opens a cupboard and discovers a stack of plates. The next cupboard door is stubborn, and he finds the hinge is broken. He can recall her voice now.

'Cosmo!' Her tone alone made him put down his postal bag heavily. 'The cupboard needs fixing,' and he sat down, exhausted, and put his feet up on the stool.

'Take your feet off the chair and find a screw.' At this he reluctantly dropped his feet to the floor again and relinquished his ease.

It had been a difficult morning. Old Grigoris had received a letter from his lawyer, and it had been hard work to follow the formal language, and even harder to reply. After that, Widow Katerina could not work out her electricity bill and when Cosmo told her the amount she must pay she broke down and cried. She did not have that sort of money, she said, and her sorrow had softened his heart, and they had cried together at her predicament. Her misery was too much to witness and so, taking out his wallet, he pulled out the twenty-euro note he kept at the back for emergencies.

'I cannot take that!' she insisted. 'When would I ever be able to pay you back?' and she had cried and looked like her heart was breaking and her world was ending.

'Please, I want you to take it. A gift.'

But a gift was out of the question.

'In all my life I have never been in such a position.' She cried all the more and then she started crossing herself and asking God why He was punishing her. In the end Cosmo, used her own religion against her.

'Katerina, by the grace of God I have this money. You think He would want me to clutch it tightly all to myself?' he reasoned. Her eyes, tight from sobbing, had opened a little then, big lakes of sorrow holding just a little hope at his words.

'Make me seem better than I am in His eyes,' he implored. 'Take the money, Katerina, for it will do me good.'

'Oh no, no, I cannot. Who can say when I will be able to pay you back?' she said, but her crooked fingers opened enough for him to stuff the note into. 'I will pay you back when my pension comes,' she said.

'Please do not be in such a hurry – the longer I am in God's good books, the better for me.'

As he climbed onto his bike, old Katerina came hurrying after him, her hands cupped.

'Take these.' And she held out three eggs to him, one still with a small, soft, brown feather attached. 'My hen, she laid them this morning.'

Cosmo felt tears pricking his eyes again.

'I would love to, Katerina, but they will break on my rounds. You keep them.' And he kicked the bike stand up and hurried away.

The whole exchange, what with crying and arguing with her to take the money, had emotionally exhausted him, so, once at home with his feet up, he was loathe to move because some hinge was loose. But when did he not do his mama's bidding? With some effort, he got to his feet and shuffled to the cupboard under the stairs for his tools and spent the last of his energy searching in vain amongst washers, bits of string and wire and spanners for a screw. Finally he admitted defeat and returned to the kitchen, sat down again and put his feet up.

'What about this door?' His mama prodded him in the shoulder.

'I will do it, Mama, but it needs a screw.'

'Well, go and buy one if you don't have one.'

'Give me a moment.'

'Oh, I know your moments …'

It exhausts him just to think about it. He closes the cupboard door carefully to avoid making the situation with the hinge any worse, and he looks around the kitchen again, hoping beyond hope that food will have magically appeared. His eyes land on the letter again. Perhaps it is just his natural inclination to put things off. Perhaps this is not the best course of action this time. Maybe he should take it immediately. Maybe it won't be as bad as he thinks.

He sits at the table and turns the envelope over and over. She was the first person on his rounds that he ever read for. Thirty years ago now. The image is burnt into his mind.

The door opened so quickly after he put the letters through the box it startled him. It was only his second week on the job and he was still nervous about the possibility of making a mistake.

'Did I make you jump?' It was beautiful Maria from school. Despite living in the same village, he had seen her only seldom since he left three years ago. Once or twice in the corner shop, and once at the *laiki* in Saros, when she was laden with bags of vegetables. He had never spoken to her, not at school and not after they left. At one time, all the boys in the village had a crush on her, and she seemed far beyond his reach. Only few had the courage to ask to court her and they had no luck. Cosmo never had the courage and had to content himself with adoring her from afar. Until, suddenly, there they were, standing face to face on her doorstep, his postbag over his shoulder, and she was asking him in. He didn't ask why – he just followed her mutely to the kitchen where her mama and baba sat with a small pile of unopened letters in front of them.

'Did I do something wrong, delivered to the wrong address?'

He hurried to the table ready to gather up the envelopes, apologising for his mistake. But Maria's baba put a hand on top of the pile.

'The thing is, Cosmo, I never really paid much attention even when I did go to school.' It was Maria who addressed him, her eyelashes fluttering. He took hold of the back of the chair next to him.

'And mama and baba, what with the farm and everything, and a herd of two hundred goats – well, they didn't have much time for school either.' She would not meet his eyes now and the colour in her cheeks was heightening.

'We cannot read,' her baba barked, and both the women looked up sharply. 'There, it is said,' the baba snapped, glaring at the women, and after a brief silence Maria continued.

'So we were wondering if maybe you could take the time to read these to us. Kyrios Spiros was kind enough to do the same before he retired, and we miss his kindness. He was also good enough not to broadcast our shortcomings. You know how people can sometimes be.'

Her eyes flicked up at him at this point, and he almost felt she was reminding him of how he was teased at school for not being too clever.

'I know what it is like to be laughed at,' he replied.

'Well, I am embarrassed to ask,' she answered and then shrugged.

'We each have our strengths. The best I can do is try.'

And he hoisted his bag off his shoulder and held out his hand for the first letter. They were mostly bills. Money they could manage, Maria's mama said, 'If we know how much we owe.' And so he took the time to show them how to read a bill and where to look for the total. He wondered why his predecessor had not done the same thing. As well as the bills, there were a couple of letters from an aunt in Athens – to whom a reply must be sent, Maria's baba said. All the while, as he read and scribed, he felt her proximity. It sent electricity through his body. Why could he not have a pleasant face and good conversation – but more importantly, why was that all it took to get a girl as pretty as Maria? His heart was good, he would be loyal and he would love her dearly – surely that was worth more?

It was Maria who showed him out again that day. The boys playing football in front of the church opposite stopped their game and turned to stare.

'Thank you, Cosmo,' she whispered.

The next time he went, she was alone. Her mama and baba were working in the orchards, she said, and an amazing smell permeated the whole house.

'I am making biscuits.'

'They smell delicious.' Cosmo's mouth was watering.

With a touch on the back of a kitchen chair she invited him to sit, and then she made them both Greek coffee and put a biscuit on a plate, breaking it in half and nodding encouragingly. They dunked the biscuit pieces in unison, Maria laughing as hers almost fell in two. She got it to her mouth just in time, and Cosmo was mesmerised by her charm.

'Amazing,' he said, spraying crumbs over the table. The heat in his cheeks burnt but she simply smiled. If only he had his time again, he would not be so gauche.

It was then their friendship started – and it is a friendship, surely?

Chapter 6

In another cupboard, Cosmo finds a bag of dried beans, and he puts them in a pan to boil. Does he add chopped tomatoes now? What else went into the sauce his mama used to make? Perhaps an onion? Should he add that now too? He chops half a tomato that he finds in the fridge, which is squishy and disintegrates into mush rather than slicing as he expected, and the wet mess slides off the chopping board into the boiling water. Then he does his best to chop an onion, but the skin will not come off, and then the centre slides out as he tries to cut it.

'*Panayia mou,*' he curses. After a few more hacks, he decides he has done enough and the chunky onion pieces follow the tomato into the pot.

His friendship with Maria might have taken a different path if she had not received a letter of such callous rejection. They were not his words, but it was his mouth that spoke them and she will not have forgotten that.

How embarrassed she was, and with each word he read he could feel her pulling away, retreating inside herself. When he finished and looked up, her cheeks seemed sunken and her eyes unfocused.

'You'd better leave now,' was all she managed to say, and it felt like his ribcage cracked open and his heart leapt from his body to comfort her, but she ran through an inner door, leaving him alone in her kitchen. He let himself out.

The next day there were bills for Maria and her family, and a letter from her aunt, judging by the handwriting, but there was no answer to his knock. Nor was there the day after. On the third, her mama opened the door just wide enough to reach out a hand for the post, and then the door closed again.

There were no more letters from that same source, but it took time for the rift to heal. Maria's family did not get an abundance of letters, but each time there was something to be delivered the door opened a little wider. Over the course of the next month or so, there were a couple of bills, and a notice from the water board, and finally he was invited in to read a letter and to write a reply. But Maria's mama was there too, and Maria herself was cold and distant, a flame rising in her cheeks if she caught his eye.

Eventually there was a day when Maria was alone, and eventually there was a day when it was almost, but not quite, like old times. But those months had stretched into more than a year. He became keenly sensitive to her every mood and he died a little with each perceived rejection.

Maria had changed since hearing the contents of that letter. Her softness had gone, and in its place something hard and unreachable lived in her. She would snap at the boys playing football outside her house and had little time for conversation in the street. She was particularly critical of the priest, which was understandable, under the circumstances. This behaviour earned her a reputation for being sour, and the boys who would once have given their right arm to walk out with her began to back away and count their lucky stars.

Her isolation only increased when first her mama died and then her baba. Now she has her cats for friends and lives a solitary life.

He puts the letter on the shelf with the canister of coffee and sugar and goodness knows what else his mama stored in all the other metal containers. The tomatoes smell like they are cooking – and the onions? He can just smell the onions.

Tomorrow is not a workday. He will take his boat, a bottle of *agioritiko*, a hunk of bread and a little feta and he will fish. It makes him smile. Not the thought of going fishing, but the fact that for thirty years he told his mama he was going fishing and in all that time he caught one fish. It was a big one, too, but when he hauled it over the side it flapped and thrashed about and he didn't know what to do. He hit it with the oar and blood spurted out but this did not kill the creature. There was an old axe handle in the bottom of the boat, so, thinking he might be more accurate with that, he hit it again, releasing more blood. By the time he had bashed it another five or six times the interior of the boat was a bloodbath and Cosmo was left panting with the exertion. He would never have guessed that such a creature could have so much blood inside it, and still its tail flapped feebly in the bilge.

He still recalls the anxiety of feeling that he was caught between two evils – if he were to throw it back, the poor thing would carry on suffering out in the open water. For how long? But to kill it, he would have to hit it again and again. The inside of his little craft was red and his stomach turned. But it had to be done, so he bashed and bashed until the innocent thing flapped no more.

Of course, most men his age, just out of their youth, knew how to kill and gut a fish, but his baba never had time for him and taught him nothing. For years he wondered what he had done to deserve this, speculating that it was his short stature that embarrassed his baba, who was a tall, broad-shouldered man. But, insidiously and covertly, it was disclosed to him that his baba suspected that Cosmo was not even his child.

This knowledge cut Cosmo like a double-edged sword. On the one hand, it was a relief to know there was nothing intrinsic to him that was 'wrong', but on the other it meant he was a displaced, unwanted bastard. He never mentioned his suspicions to anyone, and over the years he came to terms with the possibility; but, without design, he alluded to it in the course of more than one conversation with his mama. His insinuations must have fitted the truth as his mama never picked up on them or denied them. That was enough of a confirmation for him, and after a while he thought no more about it. But he grew so distant from his baba that when the old man died his mama made a point of asking if he was going to the funeral.

'How would it look if you were not there?' she said, but it was a rhetorical question.

'Of course I am going, Mama – whatever made you think I wasn't going?' And she gave him a sideways look, almost as if she was trying to judge how much he knew. Mostly he didn't care, but he never said that.

Since that first fish he has continued to go fishing. At least, that was what he told his mama. It gave him a day of peace on the water, where he was unreachable and where she thought he was being useful. When the day was done and his boat neatly moored back on the tiny wooden pier, he would pop into Saros and buy a fish from the fishmonger. His mama seemed perfectly satisfied for a while. A time came, of course, when she was no longer satisfied, and then she started to put in orders, as if a fisherman can decide what he will and will not catch.

'Can you not catch some *barbounia*?'

If he had actually been landing the fish, he can see, this would have been the moment when even going fishing would have become a contentious point at home, and his days of peace on the water, dreaming and sleeping, would have been no more. As it was, he could buy any fish she wanted, and so at least one part of his life escaped her caustic criticism.

The tomatoes smell like they might be burning. Cosmo leaps from his seat and looks into the pan. The water has boiled off and they are burning black, the skins withered. He looks in the drawer for a spoon to stir the mess, a wooden one like his mama used, but there isn't one. With building panic, he looks about the room until he spots an earthenware pot with a selection of wooden items. He grabs the pot handle. It is hot.

'*Gamoto!*' he shouts, using a word he would never have dared to utter in the house when his mama was alive. The tea towel, folded neatly into a triangle, proves to be the perfect shape to hold the pan handle, and he lifts it from the heat and stirs at the tomatoes that are now sticking to the bottom. It takes a little practice to get a bean on the blunt-edged spoon, and after blowing on it he gingerly takes it between his lips and then into his mouth to see if it is cooked.

'Aw!' His teeth jangle at its hardness. 'What?'

He spits the offending bean back into the pot and, taking another, blows again to cool it, and then, gingerly this time, he tries this one.

'These are not beans, they are stones!' he says to himself. Maybe he got the wrong sort of beans. Perhaps the way he is trying to cook them is incorrect. Who knows?

His stomach grumbles in complaint and he throws the pan back onto the stove, the spoon into the sink and the tea towel onto the table. It gives him a sense of satisfaction to make the decision to go to Stella and Mitsos's eatery for lunch. Not least because it is an act she would have condemned.

'Why would you waste your hard-earned money for a plate of food there when there can always be a plate of food here?' she argued once.

'I was just going to eat there and chat with Thanasis,' he countered.

'Well, I have cooked, so you can't,' she said, and that was the first and last time the subject was discussed. He managed to eat there once or twice after that, though, and the lemon sauce that Stella poured over his chicken and chips was to die for.

'Yes!' he exclaims to the burnt pan. 'I will eat there.' And without a further thought he steps into the sunshine and hurries over to the *ouzeri*.

Chapter 7

Lunch at the eatery has become a matter of routine very quickly. Then, in the evenings, Cosmo either cuts himself a salad at home or he goes to the *kafenio* for an ouzo, which comes with a *meze* of bread, cheese and olives. His trousers have become baggy and he tightens his belt to compensate. The loss of weight gives him energy, and it has slimmed his face a little, so he has taken to shaving his chin but leaving his moustache thick and bushy. He enjoys that too – the slow awakening in the morning, taking his time over a shave. It feels a little indulgent.

The practicalities of his mama being gone, which he originally saw as insurmountable problems, have turned out to be manageable. Babis, the village's 'lawyer for the people', was quick to slink round to his house to divulge the reason for his presence at the funeral.

'Probate, Cosmo, there is no avoiding it.' And he listed the services he would be happy to perform on Cosmo's behalf, and presented his quotation.

Cosmo told him straight. 'I cannot afford that. Forget your probate.'

'But it is the law. And I like to think of myself as a reasonable man.' Babis patted his chest with one hand and leaned so far back on his chair that Cosmo thought, and even hoped, for a moment, that he might fall over.

'So here, I'll give you a discount.' Babis leaned forward and spoke quietly, as if to give the impression that his fee was very modest. 'Over twelve months. Now, I am sure that is most generous, wouldn't you say?'

Cosmo would not say so at all, but he told Babis to start the work and that he would consider the terms anyway. With this, he held the door open and bid Babis good day.

Poppy was quick to offer to wash his clothes once a week, and he is happy to give her a few euros to supplement what little she must make in her shop. He insists on paying her something – for the electricity and the washing powder, but mostly because it means he need not feel beholden to her. She is one of the sharpest, wittiest, not to mention kindest women in the village, but even so he prefers to keep things – well, manageable. So, some of his outgoings have risen in a very short period of time, but he is not concerned as he is surely making savings. The damn television is not on all day, for a start, nor the air conditioning, nor the fan in her bedroom, and there are no longer her lotto tickets to buy several times a week, and goodness knows how much he will save in time and petrol. Most surprising is the amount he is saving on groceries. The few things he needs, he buys from the village shop, rather than that endless trawling around the shops in Saros that his mama required. He is most definitely saving on his food bill, and with just one electric light on from the time he comes back from his evening at the *kafenio* until bedtime can only enhance the small fortune he is saving on electricity.

There is still the running of the orange orchards to sort out. He has done nothing about it since she died, and this is the next pressing issue, but it no longer frightens him as it once would have. Somehow, he feels more capable now than ever before, and that is also a surprise.

The other pressing issue is the letter, which he has still not delivered.

It was the forty-day remembrance service a few days ago and he even took the letter with him in case Maria was there. But when he saw her, she spoke to him in an intimate way, expressing some of her own concerns. She said that someone had stolen her clothes from her washing line and that it was not the first time. Cosmo tried to reassure her that it would just be a boyish prank.

'I feel sure it is,' Maria agreed. 'Those boys who play football. They think it is funny.'

Cosmo suggested having a word with their mamas, but Maria only exclaimed, 'Huh!' and set her mouth into a thin, hard line.

Over the years, following various encounters, the villagers have tagged her as an awkward, trouble-making, friendless woman. Every village has one, and she, the village has decided, is theirs. The children have picked up on the adults' view of her and then they, in turn, act accordingly. The way people treat her has caused her to react badly, and it has become a cycle.

Cosmo even volunteered to talk to the boys' mamas for her about her stolen clothes. But Maria responded with an emphatic 'No!' and the frown lines between her eyes gathered, and all that had remained of her beauty in her now lined and dry face was lost.

With Maria in that sort of mood, and because she had confided in him about the clothes, he was not about to offer her the letter, knowing it would cause her to push him away and isolate herself even further. So it stayed in his inside pocket, and soon he forgot it was there.

Over the following days, he delivered a bill or two to Maria, and she invited him in, making coffee as usual and taking out the tin of home-made biscuits, breaking the first in two and offering him half. Their ritual is as intimate as they get, and it is important for that reason.

His new routine of meeting Thanasis at the eatery for lunch also adds satisfaction to his days, and it has many practical benefits, too. He has quickly learnt that whatever Thanasis does not know about paying bills, keeping house and any of the smaller issues he has to deal with, Mitsos knows instead, and if both of them are stuck, Stella is sure to have the answer. These are mostly trivial matters; for example, having decided not to keep the wood by the fire any more through the summer because it took up space, he discovered he did not know where his mama kept the key for the woodshed. It was Stella who gave him the number of a locksmith.

The days are getting hotter, but to Cosmo May is a stunning month, when the heat has not yet dried everything out and the flowers are still blossoming everywhere they can. On his rounds the village is splattered with shocks of brightly coloured flowers; huge banks of them beside the road, great swathes of them climbing arches over gates, and walls cascading with blossom. He arrives at the eatery wondering if his oranges are growing just as abundantly and whether anything needs to be done about them.

He sits with Mitsos at one of the tables that are packed together on the pavement, with their blue gingham cloths.

'Have you strimmed under your oranges yet?' Mitsos asks, as if reading Cosmo's mind. In amongst the tables, breaking through the cracks in the pavement, sprouts a tree that Stella has wound round with fairy lights. Cosmo leans sideways against the trunk and traces a finger in the condensation on his beer bottle.

'You mean the long grass? Why would I do that? It will die off in a month,' he says.

'I think you'll find it won't,' Thanasis chips in.

'Your watering system will keep it lush for a while yet,' Mitsos explains. He is watching Stella, whose head is just visible inside the eatery, behind the counter. She is pouring more charcoal onto the grill.

'Do you need a hand, *agapi mou*?' he calls to her.

'No, I am fine. Cosmo, did you want sausages with your chicken today?' Stella calls back.

'Now, why would I not want sausages?' Cosmo says by way of answer.

'And for me,' Thanasis calls.

'No sense in paying for water to keep the weeds alive.' Mitsos returns to the conversation.

'I mean, you could leave them, because, as you say, eventually the sun will turn them brown, but if they dry they become a fire risk. Better just to strim them back.' Thanasis rubs his rumbling stomach.

A car slows as it approaches the square. The driver could have parked further down the road, or further up, but instead he stops right next to them, hemming them in and blocking the road. Babis jumps out.

'Well, hello. I was just going home for something to eat but this looks like a cosy group,' he says, grinning and showing his teeth.

No one answers him. Stella comes out with two plates of food.

'*Geia sou*, Babi,' she says. 'Can I get you anything, a beer?'

'I think I might have a plate of food, that looks so good.' And he takes the plate she is about to put down in front of Thanasis.

'I'll just get you yours, Thanasi,' Stella says, a smile playing on her lips. Thanasis looks at the chicken and chips that Babis is now salting.

'There is more on the grill,' Stella assures him, and she skips back inside.

'Oh, and beer,' Babis calls after her. 'What are we talking about?' He forks up some chips, dipping them in the lemon sauce.

'Oranges.' Mitsos is the one to reply.

'Ah yes. Learning the ropes, eh, Cosmo? Your mama did not let you have much to do with the farm, did she?'

Cosmo feels a surge of energy in his chest. Babis is his junior by a fair few years, and if anyone is learning the ropes in life it is him. Thanasis clinks his glass of beer against Cosmo's bottle in an obvious effort to distract him.

'*Yeia mas*!' says Thanasis encouragingly.

'*Yeia mas*,' Cosmo replies, looking away from Babis to touch glasses with his friend.

'They think they are doing us a favour by keeping things from us, but it is rarely the case.' Babis speaks with his mouth full.

Stella delivers Thanasis his food, and Babis a beer and a glass, and lingers.

'We were discussing the pros and cons of strimming under the oranges,' Mitsos informs Stella, ever the diplomat.

'Weed killer, best thing.' Babis takes a slug of beer.

'Well, perhaps we have enough chemicals these days?' Stella says and returns inside at the call of her name, to the other farmers waiting to be fed. Cosmo has noticed that lunch is her busiest time. Babis watches her go, his mouth open, ready to answer her. Cosmo can see the half-masticated food and looks away.

'I think she is right,' Thanasis says. 'We spray on this and that – we don't really know the harm we are doing.'

'Best oranges in all of Greece from around here!' Babis says defensively, waving his fork to emphasise his point.

'Yes, but at what cost?' Mitsos says. 'Highest cancer rates in Greece.'

'My uncle died of cancer,' Cosmo says. 'Who's to say that was not caused by all the stuff he used to spray on the trees.'

'You have a point. There is a high cancer rate around here. You cannot deny that, Babi, and it is always the farmers,' Thanasis says.

'Hmm, that's because all there is round here is farmers. Stella do you have any bread?' Babis calls into the eatery.

'I'll get you it.' Mitsos is on his feet before he has finished his sentence. Cosmo continues eating in silence. For a while, Stella and Mitsos used ready-cut chips and they always cooked them perfectly but recently they, or rather Stella, has gone back to hand-cut ones using village potatoes. She put the price up a little, but no one is complaining. They are the best chips he has ever tasted, golden and crispy, and the inside is not all fluffy like the ready-cut ones – instead, these actually taste of potatoes. He scoops up some lemon sauce using a chip on his fork.

'There you go.' Mitsos puts a basket of bread on the table, waves away a butterfly that threatens to land and goes back inside. Thanasis gives Cosmo a sly look. He understands why Mitsos has retreated.

A cat runs across the road from the tiny sandwich shop and begins to wind around their legs.

'Pssst, get out of it.' Babis pushes the animal away with his foot. Cosmo nips a bit of chicken between his fingers and lets his arm dangle by his side. The cat is there immediately and delicately takes the morsel.

'So I take it you will not be spraying with chemicals, Cosmo?' Babis puts his knife and fork together and rubs his hands on his extended belly. He has on a very clean white shirt, but one of his fingers must have touched the chicken fat because now there is a greasy streak.

'As far as I know, your mama never did spray the oranges after your baba died,' Thanasis recalls. He is a slow eater. He savours his food and waits between mouthfuls.

'Couldn't afford to after he was dead.' This was one of the few things his mama had to say about the oranges. Each year, she would state that they did not have the money for the chemicals they needed for the oranges to fatten – the chemicals that probably killed her husband – but the way she said it, it always sounded as if he, Cosmo, should do something about it. On his wage there was not much he could do, so each year the time would come when she would moan, and he would let her, and then it passed. Then, later in the year she would complain that there was not enough money to spray the oranges with copper sulphate to keep them on the trees longer to take advantage of the selling price going up as January gave way to February. In all, the oranges seemed to be more trouble than they were worth. She said she got little money for them anyway, but she never said how much. Well, he will give it one year, see what he can do, and if the income is too small to be worthwhile he will live off his postman's wage, maybe even sell the farmland, if anyone would want it. Yes, why not! Be free of it altogether. He lifts his beer.

'*Yeia mas!*' he says, and Thanasis looks at him enquiringly before responding.

'*Yeia mas!*' Both he and Babis drink.

'Ha – I know,' says Babis suddenly, putting down his beer. 'Sell your oranges as organic. Yes, and charge twice the price.'

'You need certification for that,' says Thanasis, shaking his head. 'No chemicals for fifteen years and no chemicals within a ten-kilometre radius!'

'Well, there's been no chemicals for over fifteen years, that's for sure,' Cosmo says.

'Right, that's me done,' Thanasis finishes the last of his beer. 'I have a donkey in foal, so I'd best get back. Come over later, Cosmo, see if it is born.' He sorts through some coins and chucks them on the table, calling inside, '*Ade geia*, Mitso!'

Cosmo shifts his chair away from the table slightly.

'So, is the probate finished?' he asks Babis by way of conversation, looking inside to see if Mitsos is going to rejoin them.

'Takes time, takes time. I will need your signature on a few papers soon, but there is no rush, is there?' Babis is picking at his teeth with a toothpick he has taken from the holder for the salt and pepper pots.

Cosmo feels in his pocket for money. He is out of change, so he pulls out some papers from the top pocket of his jacket and finds a twenty-euro note. Normally he would wait for Mitsos or Stella to come out, but on this occasion he decides to go in to pay. He leaves his plate, his beer bottle and the papers from his pocket on the table.

Inside, both Stella and Mitsos are laughing at a joke someone has told, and it takes a moment for Stella to see him, but when she does she is quick.

'I would have come out,' she says as she hands him his change.

'Thanks, Stella.' He pockets the coins and steps back into the heat of the day. Tomorrow he will eat inside, where it is much cooler.

'Looks like you forgot to deliver one!' Babis says, and he taps at the papers Cosmo left on the table. The letter to Maria, in that scrawling handwriting, is on top, creased, corners bent and looking very worn. Cosmo's next step falters.

'You'll be getting the *sack* if you don't deliver them!' Babis laughs at his own joke and then he abruptly stops and a deep frown lowers his eyebrows.

'Actually, you don't have any letters that you are meant to be delivering to me tucked away somewhere, do you? Only, I am constantly expecting official correspondence – you know, with my work.' His voice is suddenly pompous but his frown does not lift.

'No, of course not!' Cosmo's voice comes out squeaky and high. He reaches to gather his bits of paper but Babis has picked Maria's letter from the top and is swinging it by one corner between finger and thumb.

'Actually, this could be good timing. I could deliver the letter on your behalf and that would be a very sweet introduction to Maria Pikrokardou' – he reads her name from the envelope – 'as I don't believe she has made a will yet.'

'No.' Cosmo stands abruptly and snatches the missive back. Once it is safe, he tries to recover himself. 'Er, best not, as I believe regulations state every letter has to be delivered by an official postman.'

'Yes, but at least if I took it, it *would* be delivered.' Babis stands and wipes his hands and mouth on a napkin. 'But if not me, then best you do it, Cosmo, else how can we trust the mail?' He picks up his car keys.

'Did you enjoy that, Babi?' Stella comes out with a till receipt that she gives to Babis, and whilst he is distracted Cosmo hurries away.

Lying in bed that night, Cosmo reluctantly admits to himself that, of course, Babis is right. He should have delivered that letter straightaway. It is his job, his responsibility

– and it is not his place to make judgements, however much hurt the letter might cause Maria.

As he tosses and turns, an even more sobering thought occurs to him. Someone else knows about the letter now – what if Maria were to discover that he has withheld it? That might be even worse, might damage their relationship permanently. She would not trust him after that!

These thoughts keep Cosmo awake much of that night and the next, leaving him sluggish and bad-tempered.

Chapter 8

With the letter in his pocket again, and knowing what he must do, lunch at Stella's is not the pleasant experience it usually is, and he pushes the chicken around his plate with his fork. He resolves to deliver the letter and starts in the direction of her house, but the clock strikes three, reminding him that it is *mesimeri* and not a time to be calling on anyone's house. With some relief, he turns back towards his own house. He will deliver it after five, when the day begins to cool and the villagers surface again.

When he awakes at six from a surprisingly refreshing afternoon's sleep, Babis's threats do not seem as powerful as they did, and he decides to give himself one more day to think very carefully about how he can read the letter to Maria without alienating her, sure as he is of its contents.

Before the sun is fully over the horizon, and while the whitewash of the cottages still has a bluish tinge, Cosmo is already under his orange trees wielding the strimmer Thanasis lent him last night. Cosmo spied the machine when he went over to see the new donkey foal trying to find its feet. He is a little groggy now as the easy conversation resulted in a game or two of *tavli*, and a glass or three of ouzo, sitting on upturned orange crates either side of a half-barrel that serves as a table under Thanasis's own orange trees. Cosmo mops his forehead. It is not hot yet but he is sweating profusely.

'Too much ouzo,' he chuckles to himself and he continues to strim. The contraption hangs from a strap over his shoulder. It is awkward and he is not used to manual labour.

'Who on earth did you get to do this for you, eh, Mama?' He looks up at the deep-blue sky between the orange trees, and swats at a fly. He would indeed like to know who she used and how much they charged, but there is also a part of him that would like to shake off the label of 'laziness' that the village has pinned on him. He knows he is being a little stubborn: Mitsos or Thanasis would have given him the name of a worker, or he could have chosen one of the men who loiter around the square in the morning – although there are not so many to be seen these days.

He looks more closely at a deep, shiny leaf on one of the trees, where a ladybird has landed, her wings still showing, extended below her bright red shell.

The Russian illegal immigrants have all gone since the downturn in the economy, and so have the Bulgarians and Romanians. There are only a couple of Pakistanis left, who have been here for years. One of them, he knows, is called Mahmout, but he finds him shifty, always grinning, and that alone is enough to put Cosmo off hiring him.

He slaps at another fly and looks back at the work before him, and he wonders what he should do with the dried grass once he has cut it all down. He will have to rake it all up, no doubt, and then what – burn it? Or does he leave it on the land to work back into the soil? That must be a fire risk, to let it lie there all summer, which defeats the object of strimming it.

He switches off the machine, accepting that the task is too much for him. The sudden silence makes his ears ring, then the sound of the cicadas takes over and, from somewhere within the trees, the rasp of a jay can be heard. To his left, far away, are goat bells. They could be Mitsos's goats, or Nicolaos's, or Grigoris's. He turns around to survey his progress and his shoulders drop as he realises how little ground he has covered. He has done a good job of strimming a path along the fence, but the grass is still long under the trees. It looks like he has given the place a bad haircut!

'It is hard to get under some of the trees where the branches hang so low,' he mutters to himself. 'Ah, but that will be great for the picking season.'

He bends his knees a little and leans back with his face skyward, his hands rubbing at the small of his back. When should he prune the trees? Is that done now, too? Because if so, it would be easier to do that first.

He steps forward, readying himself for another onslaught on the weeds. A branch catches at his arm and tears a thin jagged line along the surface of his skin.

'Ow!' He examines the damage. The line is red but not bleeding, and he rubs at it and glares at the offending branch. There are oranges hanging from it: hard green balls no larger than his thumbnail. If he were to cut this branch, he would lose a couple of dozen oranges. Multiply that by the number of trees in the orchard – if he were to prune all the low ones now – and that would be a good amount of fruit lost. He will not prune them now even if you are supposed to: it would be madness.

The sun has risen higher and a glance at his watch tells him it is time to go into Saros to collect the mail. He cannot remember the last time he was so happy to climb on his bike to do just that, but today anything would be a welcome break from strimming. The strimmer itself is left leaning against a tree.

The familiar journey to Saros feels different this time as he peers into the orchards either side of the road with different eyes. He notices which have been cleared of weeds and which haven't, which have been neatly pruned and which have been allowed to run wild. He makes a point of looking out for any signs of pruning – branches on the ground or raw ends of branches – but he finds none, and concludes that this is definitely not the season to prune. It feels like a relief: he does not need more work. He will go without his afternoon sleep today and carry on strimming, and maybe by the evening he will have made enough progress to justify an ouzo and a game of *tavli* with Thanasis at the *kafenio*. He could always ask Thanasis when the oranges are pruned, but – well, even though he probably knows Thanasis better than anyone else, he still feels a bit embarrassed to admit he doesn't know something so fundamental.

Thanasis, on his smallholding on the other side of the village, his brows knitted together, is feeling Coco's leg. The throbbing pulse has definitely gone. Her foot is not hot and now he wonders if he overreacted to the sight of her swollen hoof and the roll of fat on the side of her neck. She is a sweet, gentle beast, but no longer young, and that will be why she was dumped. The young donkeys nip and jostle each other, but Coco just likes to snooze. She exudes a sense of peace and he is delighted that she does not have laminitis and is not in pain. Her eyelids droop.

'Aren't you, my lovely, just a little tired?'

Her head hangs over the fence and her eyes are closed, lashes flickering at the flies. A game of *tavli* would be nice right now, but it is early. Cosmo will not be finished for hours. Maybe he will clean out the donkey barn whilst it is still relatively cool. If only he could teach donkeys to play *tavli*, his world would be complete. After patting Coco's neck and kissing her forehead, he leaves her and picks up the broom and the shovel. The vegetable patch is doing well this year so far, and bagging the surplus manure was a good idea. He has a few regular buyers from the village now, and at a euro a bag everyone is happy. The flies rise in a cloud off the manure as he enters the barn.

At the depot in Saros, everyone is busy. It has been two months since Cosmo's mama died; for a while everyone treated him a bit more carefully, but now they are back to normal, mostly ignoring him. He silently collects the mail and heads off. Some days he sorts through the letters, putting them in order at the depot, and other days he goes back to the village and does it on his kitchen table. Some of the farms are a long way out of the village itself; some are up past the monastery and, on occasion, he has not attempted to deliver letters there the day they arrive, instead waiting one or maybe even two days to see if there will be more letters so he can deliver them all together. Since Babis's goading, he has decided he will not do that any more. He will deliver any letter the day it arrives. Maria's letter is the one exception, and the envelope is now stained brown where he spilt a cup of coffee on it at home last night as he staggered to bed, and now it altogether looks like it has been trodden into the wayside and retrieved. He is not sure which is worse now: its lateness or its condition.

The drive back to the village is pleasant, the flow of air keeping him cool. His jacket has been abandoned for the summer, as has his helmet. It is far too hot for that. Besides, he only pootles along, at no speed at all, really.

At home he puts the water on to boil. He watched Theo at the *kafenio* carefully one day to see how the coffee should be made and he has been practising ever since and, he thinks, he is becoming very good at making it now. Whilst the water is coming to the boil he lets the letters cascade out of his bag onto the table and begins to make tidy piles in the order of his route. He stops to add the coffee to the water and then he watches and waits until it is done and takes his small cup of the intense stimulant to the table.

The job has changed over the years. There used to be just letters, mostly handwritten and not many of them. As time passed and people became better educated, the number of letters increased and his sack became heavier. Then the computer took over, with the immediacy of email and texting. At one point his job dwindled to the point where he wondered what he would do when the post office closed. He was preparing himself for that when, slowly, the delivery of parcels began to dominate. Bigger parcels became more frequent, and that was when they introduced the notices that he drops off in their stead to say there is a large parcel and the recipient must go to the post office at Saros to pick it up. Internet shopping had become the way, and while his sack grew heavy with the smaller packets, delivery notices dominated the letters.

There are no small parcels today, but there are many delivery notices. He has a ball of elastic bands he uses to group the letters together, all those for a given street in one pile. The elastic-band ball grows smaller as he sorts and bigger again as he delivers. Most of the streets and lanes in the village do not have names and the houses do not have numbers. Once, many years ago, someone came up with the idea of numbering each house in the village, starting with one and just going around assigning consecutive numbers, but since then so many houses have been built in between that they have given up that system, as it stopped making any sense. Cosmo knows which letter goes where by name. He knows where everyone lives, and he does not need addresses.

He is quite enjoying himself this morning. The exertion first thing in his orchard has given him energy rather than draining him and he feels ready to meet whatever the day will bring. He is even ready to face Maria with the letter.

'No!'

The sound that escapes him echoes round his small kitchen and back again.

'Nooooo.' The second sound is more of a whine. He puts his finger on the corner of an envelope he has spotted and slides it out of the stack. Sure enough, he is not mistaken: the handwriting is the same and it is addressed to Maria.

For a moment all he can do is stare. Two so close together is unusual, but not unprecedented. Did the first one say something different? Did the writer give an address, expecting an answer?

He dances up to the stained and creased envelope that he has put on the shelf with the coffee and sugar. Today was going to be the day he delivered and read it to her. He had made his mind up, he was ready, he really was, and with the energy his early-morning activity had given him he felt he could accomplish anything. But now? With two?

'Damn you, whoever you are!' He addresses the letter. 'You play with people's lives and you haven't even got the courage to sign your name!' With a sneer on his lips, which would be hidden from any onlooker by his overgrown moustache, he shoves the new envelope behind the coffee jar, so it is only just visible. He puts the stained one with it and tuts and huffs his disregard as he sorts the rest of the letters, standing at the table as if there was some hurry.

Once he is out on his bike, the two letters sit in the front of his mind. His is still huffing to himself and his postbag is digging into his back. He grumbles even more loudly as he heads to the school, where he begins his rounds. Across the road from the school, a cluster of tall cypress trees casts a welcome shade, and today there is something moving beneath them. A young man he thinks he recognises is talking to a girl, who is leaning against one of the trunks. The man's hand is on the trunk above her head and she has tucked hers behind her back so she can push herself off the trunk and let herself rock back. The youth leans forward slowly as if waiting for a rejection, but when it does not come, he becomes bolder and kisses the girl full on the mouth.

With a screech of brakes and a swerve Cosmo just misses the streak of a black-and-white cat that races across the road in front of him.

'Panayia!' he exclaims, but the image of the tender kiss he has just witnessed has not been erased by the drama. All those years his mama insisted that she should be enough for him – how could she ever have thought that? In his twenties he had not believed her and he had

courted – well, sparked up friendships – with a couple of girls, but his mama had been so condemnatory, finding fault with both the girls and their families and generally making both him and the girls feel so uncomfortable that it had been simpler not to make the effort. It wasn't as if talking to them came easily anyway. He couldn't hide his shyness and it seemed he had little to say, so in a way it felt like his mama had given him the easy way out. He had an excuse not to make the effort. As his youth passed and she repeatedly told him how lucky he was to have a mama as devoted to him as she was, he almost believed her, and apart from the occasional biological urge he was content – or at least, he considered himself so. But age brings wisdom, and her death has delivered clarity and a new perspective, and he is beginning to believe that she was wholly wrong and selfish in maintaining his single status.

'You were a selfish, self-absorbed woman,' Cosmo says out loud as he pulls up outside Sakis's house with a whole handful of letters. Saying these words out loud feels surprisingly good. He stops and straightens his back.

'Selfish, self-absorbed woman,' he says again. A grin forms on his lips, but in his chest, anger bubbles. He stuffs the letters harshly through the letterbox and returns to his bike.

None for Anna across from Sakis today. Anna. Now, she is a woman who never liked his mama. She never said so outright, but she said on a number of occasions over the years, 'No matter how much you love your mama, she is not enough. A man should have a wife.'

She would twist her thin gold band around her crooked finger when she said this. But Cosmo, in turn, twisted the logic and doubted whether this rule applied to him because he was in fact unsure that he *did* love his mama. Mostly she just irritated him, and at other times she reduced him to feeling slow, lazy and incapable. So useless, who would want him as a husband anyway?

'You are a fine man, with a good heart. Find yourself a girl,' Kyria Anna repeated. But Cosmo knew that it wasn't the inside of someone you see when you are thinking of courting, and if there was anything 'fine' about him it would certainly take some discovering.

He hitches his jeans over his shrinking hips. Well, he is less tubby than he was, and with his shaven chin he looks better than he did. It has even crossed his mind to shave off his moustache.

He first stopped shaving in his early twenties when he noticed his double chin.

'Too much *pastichio*,' his mama commented, but she continued to pile his plate high and admonish him for his ingratitude if he did not eat the lot.

'A decision made, then,' he tells himself. The moustache must go and then he will see better who he is.

The rest of his morning is uneventful and he returns home earlier than usual. He has time for a bite to eat at Stella and Mitsos's, and then he will continue clearing the weeds in the orchard, if it is not too hot.

He is about to put his empty postbag on the back of one of the kitchen chairs when he looks at the hooks by the door. Her coats and aprons occupy more than half of the hooks, and without thinking he rips them from where they hang and throws them in a heap on the floor, and then takes a large black rubbish sack from the kitchen drawer. He stuffs the lot in, ties up the top and tosses it out of the back door. Then he casually takes his postbag and hangs it on one of the three empty hooks.

'Ahh, there.' His satisfaction elongates the words. He steps back to admire the view and rubs his chin. His fingers creep up and play in his moustache, which brings about his second burst of activity. The kettle is put on to heat water, his shaving bowl is brought, his razor is found and a mirror is stood on the table, resting against the pale-green wall.

'White.' He decides on the wall colour as the kettle comes to the boil. He pours the water into the bowl, and begins the process of ridding himself of his thirty-year-old moustache to see who it is hiding. It takes longer than he expects, and more concentration than he anticipated, but after a great deal of close-up work in the mirror he sits back to take a good look at his whole face.

'Oh.' He does not recognise himself and he stares some more. There is no trace of his baba in his face, and his mouth is too generous to be his mama's. His eyebrows are rather bushy, but apart from that it is a nice face.

'Why have I been hiding behind all that itchy, scratchy hair all these years?' he asks himself, and he smiles at the stranger in the mirror. The stranger smiles back and he decides he likes the stranger. The stranger has an honest face that looks as though it has humour, and there is kindness in the eyes, which is accentuated now the harsh line around the mouth is gone.

He runs a hand through his hair, which touches his collar at the back. Perhaps it is time for a haircut too, and maybe, what with his belt being on the last notch, he needs to buy new trousers.

'Yes, indeed,' he says to himself.

But then, in the reflection, on the shelf, he notices not one but two letters addressed to Maria, and the stranger's smile is gone. He knows in his heart what they will say, but why two, why so close together? He could deliver them and refuse to read them, but that would be just as unkind as reading them. They are not going to make her happy and she will know it too, so maybe delivering them but refusing to read them *is* the answer. He can even say he will not read them because they will make her unhappy, but why say what she knows already? He could just slip them under her door and say nothing. Yes, that is a good solution.

He stops looking at them through the mirror and turns to take them down from the shelf. If these letters had never come, how would he have courted Maria? His insides shrink and a small voice lets him know that he would have been no braver. The things he would have had to say would still have been left unsaid. His stomach lurches: has he used these letters as an excuse, a simple reason not to face doing what he found hard to do, a veil over his own cowardice?

Chapter 9

He stands open-mouthed at his own thoughts.

'Is that the truth, eh, Cosmo?' he addresses himself. The second letter is not sealed well either, the glue on the aging envelope long gone. It takes no effort and leaves the envelope unmarked as he flicks it open. The yellowing, lined paper with the water stain in the top corner seems so familiar, like a toothache that won't go away. He reads,

There are days when I think I might have the nerve to tell you of my love, but if you have not noticed me all these years then it is not meant to be.

He stops reading. It is the same as all the others; the writer doesn't even vary his language or his sentences any more. In the first few years the letters carried more hope, more promise that the writer might actually declare who he was, offer her something more real, but as time has passed they have all begun to sound just like this one – accepting that his love is unrequited and therefore requiring no answer. But indeed, how could Maria reply when the sender never puts an address, never even scrawls his name at the bottom?

'What is the point?' Cosmo asks. Some insect scratches in the roof beams, breaking the silence.

It was not intended, of course, but one thing these letters have done is stop him declaring his own love to Maria. Or rather, not so much the letters, as Maria's reaction to them. But it was not these letters that made her withdraw so deeply into herself: it was that first letter from a different author, the rejection letter itself. That was such a devastating blow to Maria that it is possible she will never recover, being as delicate and defensive in her nature as she is. But it is the love letters that have shredded his hope, acting as they have like a dripping tap, reminding poor Maria of the first.

Cosmo shakes his head. He can still feel her pain on hearing him read the rejection letter. Her face first became hard, emotionless, then slowly cracked and distorted at the words as he read them until she was unrecognisable in her distress. She crumbled before him, her beautiful young mouth twisted into an ugly grimace, her brow contracted into a hundred lines, her eyes expressing the pain that her heart was feeling, and it broke his own heart to see her in such agony. He hated himself for being the messenger, and although of course he did not know it at the time, what he saw in her face was a glimpse of how time would distort her beauty to reflect her changed feelings, from soft and beautiful to bitter and hard, her face twisted by her outlook. Poor Maria.

He puts the letters one behind the other, back behind the sugar jar, and sits heavily at the table. That day, the day the rejection letter arrived, had been like any other. He had been doing the job for nearly two years by then, and with the cockiness of youth he thought nothing could surprise him or catch him off guard. He had read letters telling old men that their sisters had died, then watched them crumple and cry like children before listening to every memory that could be recalled of their poverty-stricken childhoods. He had read letters to women from defiant daughters engaged to unsuitable men and heard a tirade of language that shocked him. He had read of births and joined in with the listeners' delight, read of children moving abroad and sympathised with those left behind, and read of businesses going bust and become wiser for knowing the details. What had he not had to impart in the brief time he had been employed to deliver the post? That day had been like any other, quieter if anything, and so he arranged that Maria would be his last call. This took away all time constraints, so if he had the chance he could stretch out his time with her; maybe one coffee could become two.

With the energy of youth, he knocked on her door with a little embellishment, a quick rhythm, and she opened it with a smile. It is funny how these meaningless moments become forever impressed on the mind when they are the forerunners to events that should never occur. He knew her smile was not all for him. Not much can be kept secret in a village and the news that Maria had started to walk out with one Nektarios from Saros had spread quickly, and Cosmo had watched her blossom under this man's attention. Of course, this made it impossible for her ever to be romantically involved with him, Cosmo, but he had never really expected that would happen anyway. He was just pleased for her. It was generally agreed that she was beautiful, and since the rumours started she had begun positively to glow. It was whispered by the old women that Nektarios was from a good family and that he would soon propose. Maria walked with her back a little straighter and held her head a little higher. There had been a softening to her features as well, as if a weight had been lifted from her, and there was a contentment about her as if her future, away from the uncertain life that is a farmer's lot, felt assured for her.

It had seemed inevitable that someone from outside the village, someone worthier, would gain her love. After all, what did the village boys, or even Cosmo himself, have to offer? Nothing. But he hoped that maybe they could continue to be friends, if friends indeed they were at this point.

He was also aware that if this rich boy did make his offer then Maria was bound to move to Saros to live in the family house – or perhaps his parents would buy a new home for the couple. Would Cosmo even see her again?

Such were his thoughts as he made his trill of a knock and she invited him to read her letters to her.

'How were your rounds today?' she asked, holding the door open. She was alone today. Occasionally her mama was there, but more often than not both parents were tending the olive trees or working in the polytunnels where they grew aubergines and cucumbers.

'Much the same. I can smell something good.' He hung his bag on the back of a wooden chair and sat at the well-scrubbed kitchen table.

'Biscuits.' Maria took the *briki* from a nail in the wall and filled it with water from the tap. She lit the single-burner gas stove on the old marble counter by the cracked and stained marble sink and set the little pan on top to make coffee. He watched her long, supple limbs as she reached for the tin of coffee on the high shelf. How many times had he watched her do that and fought the urge to stand and offer his help, to stand behind her and reach past her? If she turned in such a position their faces would be so close.

But he remained seated and the coffee was made without his help. The biscuits came straight from the oven and as she broke the first into two pieces it crumbled and steamed. Maria passed him half and blew on her fingers to cool them. He wanted to take her hand and blow on her fingertips for her. He almost saw himself doing it, but her eyebrows were raised, questioning, looking towards his postbag.

'Two today. One a phone bill but the other – well, here, you can see.' He passed her the letters.

'Oh,' she said at the sight of the flourishing hand that had addressed the second letter. She delicately tore open the envelope and after a brief uncomprehending glance handed it back.

'Who is it from?' she asked, a little smile playing on her lips.

'Er …' He turned the sheet over and then looked at the second sheet. Oh, Kyrios Nektarios.' He added the polite form of address, joining in with her charade.

The talk about Nektarios and Maria was on everyone's lips. For the village, it was a Cinderella story. He was from one of the richest families around, and with Maria being just a poor farmer's daughter from a village their possible engagement had spread like wildfire, bringing disappointment both to the girls who had been hopeful that they might catch

Nektarios and the boys who were pining for Maria.

Cosmo then looked at the postmark – Athens – and just a tiny knot started in his stomach.

'Oh.' Maria wriggled on her seat at the sound of Nektarios's name and tried to veil her excitement. 'Do please read it.'

Her face lit up and Cosmo wondered how it must feel to have the power to affect someone in that way.

He smiled too, ignoring the intuitive tightening in his gut. He liked imparting good news and happy tidings. People treated him as if it was he who had made wonderful things happen.

'Dearest Maria,' he started, clearing his throat. 'Our courtship has been a wonderful rush of nothing but good feelings.' He glanced at Maria, who was looking past him, away into the distance, her eyes shining and alive.

'How fortunate we have been that we have stepped out together so often and so freely. Your parents have been very generous with your time. It was always such a pleasure to spend those hours with you, but I did wonder, on occasion, at how free they were with such a perfect treasure.'

His eyes flicked towards Maria again, who, although still looking into the distance, now wore a small frown.

'Read on,' she commanded.

'You knew of my impending trip to Athens, and now I am here. With my future before me, it is amazing how my perspective on life has changed. If you were here I feel sure that you would understand.'

Cosmo coughed then and was about to take a sip of coffee to free his throat when Maria spoke again.

'Read on, read on.' Her voice was quite sharp.

'In fact, I cannot help but feel that you would not like life in Athens. It is fast-paced and the women here are so very polished.' Cosmo did not dare to look at Maria at this point, and his cheeks were on fire. He forced himself to go on.

'I think it would be a merciful thing for you if you never had a reason to come to Athens, so opposed to your nature do I think you would find the place. In fact, I am sure, if you were ever to come here, it would only end in unhappiness for you, being so far from your little village and your farming family.'

Cosmo looked up now, to see Maria's face crumple. Little sobs began to escape her, and he was not sure of the best thing to do, so he did what was easiest: he read on.

'I want you to know that it is not because of the rumour that you offered no dowry, although I was somewhat surprised at that.

After all, it is not as if your family's land is small. But I will not talk of that.'

The sobbing became more audible but Maria was doing her best to hold everything inside. Cosmo forced out each word in turn.

'So I thank you for your kind friendship. I wish you well in your future life as I know you will wish me in mine.'

And the letter ended very formally indeed.

He carefully folded the letter back along its creases and was lifting his head to offer Maria his commiserations and to give her any sort of comfort he could when he heard a door bang and looked up to find the kitchen empty.

He waited a good half an hour to reassure himself that she was not coming back to the room and then he very quietly let himself out.

Her door was not opened to allow him to read any letters for some time, and in that time she changed. When he finally saw her face to face long enough to see what had become of her, he found a hardness that had never been there before, and in her voice a sharpness and in her words a cynicism. After that, she was very critical of the papas in the church house opposite her own home and she was very short with the boys who played football in front of the church. In fact, anyone who came into her firing line became a target for her now-angry nature, and this only increased with time and doubled after her baba's death. After a while, she was seldom seen outside the boundaries of her own yard.

Eventually the door was opened to Cosmo. First, just so she could take the letters. Then, nearly a year later, he was allowed in, and over some considerable time coffee became part of the process of reading her mail to her again. She slowly allowed their conversations to grow more personal but it never became the friendship it had once been. After all, it was he who had brought the news and witnessed her humiliation and her grief. He was her permanent reminder.

Also, too few letters came that needed reading to allow him to make any consistent impression on her, and there were seldom any really positive, joy-filled letters to give him the chance to make up for the damage he had done as the reader of her rejection letter.

Then came the first of these futile love letters. Had the timing been intended to do harm to his relationship with Maria, it could not have been more perfect.

The first letter had been very bold, and for a moment he wondered, maybe even hoped, if it might be the cure Maria needed.

He can still recall how it started. *Now your other suitor is out of the way I can confess my love*, it had begun, or something like that, and he had looked at her with hope. But how wrong he had been to think this might be what Maria needed. The poor girl had physically recoiled. He faltered and wondered if he should continue, but surely she would have told him to stop if that had been her wish.

How had it gone on? Something like *But if it is meant to be then you will see me and know*. He read to the end and then she asked him twice who it was from. He replied twice that it was not signed, but his words brought no smile to her lips: only a frown to her brow.

Then she said, 'I think you'd better leave now.' Her voice was cold and hard and he stood and walked out. Her door remained shut to his knock for some considerable time after that.

In time, she did start to open the door to him again and he did start to read her letters, and she made coffee and offered biscuits. But at the rate he saw things progressing it would be years before the pain retreated enough for them to become closer, and he was right. It has been years, nearly thirty of them. Two steps forward, then a love letter turns up and it's one step back. A less patient man would have given up. Age might have taken away much of her physical beauty and she might have a reputation for being bad-tempered, sharp and aloof, but she is still long of limb and graceful and she is still his Maria. He understands. It is only recently, in the last year maybe, that he could honestly say that they are at least comfortable with each other again.

But now, to shake all that up, to rock this so carefully moored boat, there is one of these damned anonymous, pointless love letters again.

Chapter 10

As he steps out of the front door, the heat of the summer reminds Cosmo of the bread oven in the yard to the side of the house: of peering in, as a young boy, to see if the loaf had risen. The oranges are hard and green, and still very small. Cosmo feels a little disappointed that they are no bigger, but he is relieved to see that they are the same as everyone else's.

It is only August and he has called someone out to service the fans already, and he feels just a little smug. He has not waited, as so many farmers do, until he actually needs the fan to work to queue up with all the other farmers for the same service – from the same man!

How many times has he sat in the *kafenio* and heard that refrain!

'Ach, but the man said he could not come until next Tuesday. What if there is a frost before then?' – from one man.

'No frost is forecast' – from his neighbour.

'Forecasts! Who trusts them?'

'Count yourself lucky. He told me next Thursday. It sounds like you are part of my problem, friend.'

'Yes, and I wonder who is part of mine.' And the first farmer would look around at his friends in accusation. It is good-hearted banter on the whole, but they all know there is a slice of truth in it. Well, Cosmo has made sure he will miss all that.

His mama had three fans strategically positioned around the orchards. Huge things they are, ten metres tall and with blades wider than Cosmo's outstretched arms. They won't be used until January or maybe even February, when the frosts come, but he will be ready. The fans' job is to blow the warmer air from ten metres up down into the trees, raising the temperature just enough to stop the oranges – which by that time will be heavy and fat – from freezing and falling off the trees.

It turns out he was wise to get them serviced. The mechanic calls down to say that there is a fault with the last of the fans.

'You want me to fix it while I am up here? I couldn't put it in with the service fee, I'm afraid, and the price will depend on how long I am up here …'

Cosmo shades his eyes from the sun and peers up at the man.

'Unless of course you want to fix it yourself?' the mechanic calls down. 'It's not tricky, so long as you are okay with heights.' He laughs.

Cosmo frowns. He called the man out to service the fan, and he has found a problem. So why is he now saying it is not part of the service? Is this normal? The serviceman that the other farmers use recently retired, apparently. This man, Michalis, isn't from the village; maybe he's from Saros, or the next cluster of houses. Cosmo has seen him a few times in Theo's *kafenio* and he knows it does not take long to hear of a man's reputation there. Maybe Michalis has heard of his unwarranted reputation for being lazy and is exaggerating the scope of the job to earn a few more euros?

Well, if Cosmo proves that label wrong enough times, perhaps it will change. Michalis's can be one voice to the contrary at least. Besides, it will save him a euro or two. Yes, he will do it himself.

'Oh no, no, no. I will do it.' Cosmo injects a chuckle into his reply. 'Don't bother yourself, my friend.'

'Are you sure? I think it just needs the brushes replacing.' The serviceman's toes shift on the metal ladder that runs up one side of the pylon on which the fan is mounted. One of his arms is hooked through the top rung, leaving both hands free to deal with the mechanics.

'No problem,' Cosmo shouts up, 'if it is just the brushes, whatever they do. It sounds easy enough. He watches as the man climbs down.

From the bottom of the metal column it looks a long way to the top, but the ladder is like any other. In his hand he grips the replacement brushes. Cosmo ordered them yesterday, and the man in Athens put them on the bus, and he picked them up from the bus station in Saros this morning when he went for the mail.

He starts to climb with energy, and as soon as he is above the trees he looks down at his orchard, laid out around him, a carpet of green, as if he could step off and walk out across it. He feels tempted to do this and then terrified that he has had this thought. He pushes himself upwards. He will be fine if he keeps three points of contact at all times: two hands, one foot; two feet, one hand.

As he climbs, his grip becomes tighter and tighter. He feels high up now, but he knows he is only twice the height of an orange tree and he forces himself on. Above him, the ladder is twisted. It is still welded tight to the shaft but there is a kink in the metal and this makes him wonder how safe it is. Then he starts to see the rust, in corners where the rungs meet the uprights, and his breath leaves him and his heart thuds in his ears and before he knows what he is doing he is on the ground again.

'Are you a man or a boy?' he berates himself, catching his breath, and he steps back to put the height of the fan tower in perspective. It really isn't very high. 'As a boy you would have climbed it without a thought.' And with this, he tells himself to ignore the dangers and to see it as an adventure.

This approach makes the ascent no easier, and it is an hour later before Cosmo is finally hanging from the top of the fan pole, having conquered his fear, and fighting to get the cover off the motor in the relentless August sun. He is wondering if not getting the man to do the job for him was wise. Sweat is running in his eyes, making it impossible to see, and with one arm through a ladder rung and his other hand holding a spanner that he has locked on to a bolt, he needs a third hand to wipe his brow.

'*Gamoto!*' He swears and pauses to take a breath. He can see the extent of his orchard from up here, and the one next to it and the one beyond that, all the way across the plain to the foot of the mountains that rise majestically on all sides in a horseshoe ending at Saros and the sea. Towards Saros, the trees thin out, and then, from this vantage point, the town itself can be seen: a patchwork of terracotta roofs at the head of the wide sparkling bay. His own village sits on a finger of blue that has crept inland. The cluster of houses he calls home is a smaller patchwork than that of Saros, with a pimple of a hill next to it topped with pine trees. He has never seen it from this position before.

A noise below draws his attention, and there in his own orchard he can see the Pakistani man – Hardeep – whom he hired from the village square this morning. He seems like a good man but possibly a slow worker.

The tiny figure lifts his *tsapa* and sinks it into the hard earth, and again; it rises and falls, rises and falls as he digs a channel around each tree so the water can pool and soak into the roots. Cosmo could have done that job too, but he does not have the time to do all the work himself – not as long as he has his postal job too.

But he was right to fix the fan himself. The man would have been up here for hours, and it would have cost more than he can afford. He turns his attention back to the job. If he could take the whole motor off and lower it down to the ground it would be much easier to work on. Also, he would not need to worry about dropping the nuts and bolts, or the fiddly springs that are meant to hold the brushes in place.

It soon becomes clear that the only way he can take the motor down is by first removing the heavy fan blades. These can be secured to the top rung of the ladder and left hanging there whilst he works on the motor.

'So far, so good,' Cosmo murmurs under his breath, as he climbs back up for the third time, with a rope to secure the blades. The engine comes away more easily than he expected, but it is also a good deal heavier than he anticipated. It would be useful to have a bag to put it in, so that he can sling it over his shoulder and take it down that way. Or another rope, and then he could lower it down. But he has neither, and he is tired of climbing the ladder, and so, with the motor tucked under one arm, he begins a careful descent. His feet falter on the slim metal rungs, his knuckles white with the tightness of his grip. It is slow progress and he breathes a heavy sigh of relief when his feet touch the freshly strimmed ground.

Hardeep has stopped for a rest, and who can blame him, really? He has been digging for hours in this heat. Consulting his watch, Cosmo is surprised to see the day has flown by and it is past time for his worker to leave. No wonder he seemed to be working slowly; his day was in fact done half an hour ago.

'Er, Hardeep.' Cosmo fumbles in his trouser pocket for his curl of euros, takes them out and peels off the agreed couple of notes.

'Tomorrow?' Hardeep asks, and then he turns with a flowing movement of his arm to indicate all he has done today, to demonstrate his worth as a worker. When Cosmo takes stock from the ground, and considering how long it took him to strim the same area himself, he nods, and raises his eyebrows.

'Yes, tomorrow.' Hardeep grins widely and his features relax. Cosmo is reminded of Maria all those years back, when the opening lines of Nektarios's letter brought such a pleasant change in her countenance, before the rejection. He is glad that Hardeep's happiness is not about to be spoilt; in fact, seeing the effect his offer of further work has had on the man motivates Cosmo to take an extra euro from his pocket.

'Get yourself a beer,' he says, and Hardeep actually bows. Not deeply, but there is a definite incline of his head, deeper than a nod, and Cosmo feels a heat in his neck rising into his cheeks and he turns away rather abruptly.

'Tomorrow,' Hardeep calls after him in a voice that is light and joyful.

On his drive home, Cosmo wonders about Hardeep and the other illegal workers in the village. There used to be more – Russians, Bulgarians, Romanians; many have gone since the economic crisis started. Now there are only one or two Pakistanis left. Why have they stayed? Can they not go home? Where is Pakistan, anyway?

He pulls up his bike and goes into the house, dumps the fan motor on the table and continues to his mama's room. When he was a child, his baba kept an atlas on top of the wardrobe. His fingers grope in the dust for the edge of the book. The bedroom feels lifeless and smells fusty. He mustn't leave it too long before he clears it out.

Turning the old pages on the kitchen table, he delights in the coloured blocks that represent the countries, just as he did as a boy.

Greece is pink; the village is so small it is not mentioned by name and the distance between Saros and Athens is less than the width of a little finger.

There are Bulgaria and Romania to the north, and there is the edge of Russia, but where is Pakistan? He has never wondered before, despite having delivered letters from there. The Pakistanis do not have permanent addresses in the village and he leaves their letters with Marina, in the shop.

'Pakistan, Pak-i-stan.' His finger trails further and further away from Greece, past Turkey, and Syria, Iraq, Iran, Afghanistan … And then, 'Ha, there you are. So far!'

He takes his finger away and assesses the distance. 'Halfway to China!' He whistles through his teeth. No wonder they are still here. How can they afford to go home? It's not as if they can walk back!

Where do they live, he wonders – Ali, Mahmout and Hardeep, and the others whose names he cannot remember. Hardeep has proved himself to be a hard worker, and it seems right that he should have his letters, few though they are, delivered to his home like any other man. He must ask tomorrow if there is an address. He snaps the atlas shut, and a puff of dust hovers over the table.

Chapter 11

The yard at the rear of Thanasis's little cottage is unpaved, the mud compacted hard and baked in the sun. Thanasis is examining the hoof of one of his donkeys, and he sets it gently down as Cosmo comes round the corner. The animal flicks its tail at the flies, but it doesn't open its eyes.

'Ah, what have you there?' Thanasis says, eyeing the motor under Cosmo's arm. He pulls on the halter, leading the animal back into the enclosure with the other donkeys, which stand in the shade of a huge walnut tree, eyes closed, drifting in and out of sleep.

'It's the motor from one of my fans. I need to change the brushes, apparently.'

'You're early with this job, aren't you?' Thanasis remarks, and he sweeps the leaves off a rough wooden bench under the orange trees and drags it to the centre of the yard.

'Not going to get caught out when everyone wants the serviceman,' Cosmo says.

'Ah, wise, very wise. Hang on, I'll get my tools.'

Thanasis stoops to enter the low door to his little cottage. It is one of the oldest cottages in the village, or rather just outside the village. The back of it runs parallel to the road that leads out to the next cluster of houses, and its front faces the orange orchards. Two windows are set into the plaster on one side of the door, and the whitewash is so thick in places that it has peeled off in sheets, the pieces of white settled like dandruff on the ground. The handmade terracotta tiles on the roof are covered in lichen and they sag in a graceful curve. It doesn't look like a place someone would actually live. And the gate to enter it! It is a cat's cradle of wire and bits of wood, cobbled together out of found objects. For Cosmo the gate is typical of Thanasis: functional, unconventional and innovative. At one point, Thanasis found an old *Beware of the Dog* sign, which he has wired to his makeshift gate, but to Cosmo's knowledge there has never been a dog.

Thanasis has not always been a donkey breeder. In the seventies he ran a nightclub in Saros, The Black Cat, but Cosmo was still at school when the business closed.

From inside the cottage there is a clattering sound and an expletive, and then Thanasis re-emerges with a battered and rusting toolbox.

'Right, so let's get the casing off, and we can have a look at the old brushes. You have the new ones, yes?'

Cosmo nods, and Thanasis selects a clamp.

'And then we need something like … Ah, that will do.' He puts a broken chisel next to the clamp. 'You know, this is why I gave it all up.'

'What's why you gave all what up?'

'This sort of messing about that growing oranges creates, not getting paid, and the time it takes to strim.'

'Oh, I forgot your strimmer.' Cosmo looks up from the motor.

'Good, that's another thing I should have got rid of when I sold the orchards. Just never got around to it. I don't really need it just for these.' Thanasis selects a screwdriver and points over his shoulder at the trees that surround his cottage. 'Hold the motor so it doesn't twist, will you? These screws are rusted on.'

Cosmo is sweating already.

'It's a silly game everyone round here seems to play without question!'

'Is that why you sold them? Because of messing about with stuff like this? There, put your screwdriver there.'

'That and the fight every year for a decent price. But, you know what, I think I ran too fast and I probably burnt out early. The Black Cat took it out of me. Just the day-to-day running of it. I thought it would be fun, you know, to run a nightclub. I pictured myself at the bar, chatting to the customers, hanging out. You know what I mean? Like a night out every night, but without spending. And it was fun, of course, but the bureaucracy! You wouldn't believe it! Licences, taxes, social security, stock control, accounting. Endless!'

He sighs as if the weight of the world is too much to bear. 'And the hassle with the oranges was just too much on top.'

One of the donkeys takes a deep rasping breath that sounds like the beginning of a bray but peters out before it has properly started.

'But to sell it all was pretty drastic! Have you got any oil? We might as well oil the bearings while we've got the casing off.'

'Good thinking. There in the toolbox. It was the most natural thing in the world. My cousin's kids wanted to go to university, one in France, the other in Holland, and what better reason to sell was there than that?'

'Do you think you can keep holding that, but turn this ... yes, there – ah, that's it! Do you ever regret it? You know, only having the donkeys now?' Sweat is dripping into Cosmo's eyes, blinding him, and he wipes an arm across his forehead.

'I used to want things, things I suppose people consider normal – a house, a wife, maybe even children.' Thanasis briefly chortles. 'But I think the bar showed me too much about life and I just stopped wanting anything.'

'Apart from donkeys.' Cosmo chuckles now.

'Ah, the donkeys. They are my children now,' Thanasis says. 'You laugh, I hear you, but there are many men like me. There was a man came the other day all the way from Orino Island for a donkey. Now, him I understood. I swear he was a younger version of me! All he needed was a very simple life and a donkey for company, and that man was as content as ever I have known a man to be.'

'Didn't he have a wife?'

'No.'

'Hmm, now my mama has passed, God rest her soul' – his impulse is to cross himself but his hands are occupied with the motor – 'I am not so sure man is designed for single life.'

'Well, if that's the way you feel, there is still time, man! … I think I have it! Yes!'

The screw that Cosmo is struggling with comes loose and a washer comes with it, rolling across the table and onto the floor.

'Have you never thought of getting married?' Cosmo pauses, holding up the old, worn brushes, which are now free of the motor. 'Right, let's see if we can get the new ones in.' Cosmo peers into the workings of the motor.

'There was a girl once,' says Thanasis. 'Thought about her a lot over the years but, well, it never seemed to be the right time to make my feelings known. Besides, you know how it is. Late at night you feel lonely, and need a bit of companionship, but then you wake up the next morning and you want to seize the day. A woman, at those times, with her demands for things domestic, would only be annoying. I think, perhaps, these unfulfilled ideas have become unrealistic fantasies rather than realities. Although I think a part of me still hopes.'

Thanasis begins to gather up the spanners, arranging them neatly back in the toolbox.

'Are you going to put it back up tonight, because I think we are losing the light.'

One of the donkeys has put its head over the fence, a rickety affair cobbled together out of palettes and wire. Thanasis goes over to the animal, pats its neck and leans his face in so that, for a second, they are cheek to cheek.

'Tomorrow will do. Do you wish you had spoken out?' Cosmo is curious to know what Thanasis feels about the path he has taken. It might just help him make up his own mind about what to do.

'Sometimes. Like now, for example – would it not be good if a woman came out of my cottage with a large *pastichio* straight from the oven?'

Thanasis laughs and looks over to the door, clearly picturing the scene.

'Ha! You haven't got an oven.' Cosmo packs the rest of the tools away. The sun is sinking and has softened the edges of the world, bathing everything in a pinkish hue.

'But if I had a wife then I would have an oven.' Thanasis takes a rag that is hanging on the branch of one of the trees and wipes his hands carefully. 'So, do you want to share the remains of a *spanakopita*, or shall we go to Stella's for something to eat?'

He rehangs the rag and turns to his well. With some energy he pumps the lever, and when the water arrives it spurts from the ironwork into a bucket. With his free hand, Thanasis puts a piece of guttering under the cascade, directing the flow of water to a series of half-pipes that lead through a hole in the fence and into the water trough. Cosmo has seen Thanasis do this hundreds of times but the simple ingenuity still fascinates him.

They sit in silence watching the beasts drink. In the distance, somewhere in the village, a cockerel crows, confusing the setting of the sun with its rising, perhaps.

'Stella's,' Cosmo says finally, and his friend rolls down his sleeves and they set off on the twilit road.

They eat slowly, watch the night fall, drink an ouzo or two, and then Cosmo declares he will call it a night. He did not have a sleep in the afternoon and he must be up for the post in the morning.

'Are you going home so early because you know I am about to challenge you to a game of *tavli* and you are scared you will lose?'

Thanasis is more than a little merry from the ouzo.

'If I thought you could give me any real competition I would stay for sure.' Cosmo is quick to tease him back.

'I seem to remember that it was you who didn't give me any competition the last time we played,' Thanasis says. The strange, wobbling sound of a donkey echoes across the village. The momentum builds; the crescendo has nearly arrived when it quite suddenly stops.

'Bronk. I have called that one Bronk.'

'Well, Bronk is calling you home and I must go to my bed, so I wish you goodnight, my friend.'

The village is silent as they make their separate ways home. Cosmo turns at the corner for a last look at the fairy lights wrapped around the tree outside the eatery, which cast light in a pool around the tables.

Cosmo decides it has been a good day all round. This farm work is satisfying, and tinkering with the engine with Thanasis was very companionable. He turns into his road and at the far end he can see the light of the big house off to one side behind the church. The balcony is lit and the papas is lounging there.

How often the sight of the priest has reminded Cosmo of Maria's suitor. The other girls in the village had regarded Maria with envy when she began to walk out with Nektarios, who would soon be ordained, and who would provide her with all the trappings befitting a priest's wife: a modern house, a car, an income for life and then a generous pension. And, it was rumoured, Nektarios's father had pulled strings so his eldest son would be posted to Athens immediately and would not have to spend years in some rural village. They would be married first, everyone in the village knew, and then he would be ordained, since priests may not marry once they have taken their vows. Of course, everyone also knew that he hadn't actually asked her yet, but this was surely a mere formality, and preparations had begun …

'The dirty dog!' Cosmo exclaims as he recalls all this, and he spits on the ground. 'How that must irk Maria every time she opens her door or looks out of the window to see a priest.'

He shakes his head. 'To be reminded like that, every day, of her rejection, of her spinsterhood,' he mutters to himself, and he stands and stares at the papas all lit up. She must have thought her situation was so sure. And then – the rejection letter. He lets out a breath that surprises him by turning into a burp. The food was good.

Sometime after the rejection letter, he heard that Nektarios had delayed his ordination so he could marry a rich woman from Athens. He didn't mention this to Maria, of course. It is not surprising that Maria is so openly bitter about the church and all it stands for, or that she remarks on and judges almost everything the papas does. The villagers don't understand. It is easier for them to think she is just a busybody – for that is how her actions make her appear. If only they knew the whole truth, perhaps they would understand. But it is not his story to tell, and he is unable to come to her defence, so she must bear the looks of the villagers and he must bear the things that some of them, the unkinder ones, say about her.

He still hasn't got used to coming home to find the house in darkness. Maybe he could get a timer, or a light that comes on with movement. Do those exist or has he just made them up?

'Imagine Thanasis having a fancy for a girl,' he chuckles as he heads up the stairs. It's hard to imagine his friend being anything but a very confirmed old bachelor.

Chapter 12

Usually very reliable, the bike seems to be misfiring today. It coughs and belches out black smoke as Cosmo brings it to a stop outside Anna's house. It has done this once before and his mama nagged him to get it fixed, but then the problem cleared up of its own accord. Maybe it will again.

He kicks the stand down and delivers a bundle of letters to Sakis opposite. He hesitates to leave as he can hear the musician playing his guitar, the melody drifting through the open letterbox, but as Cosmo's postbag is full today he must press on. There are none for old Anna, but he knocks anyway: he has not seen her for a few days, and it is best to check she is all right once in a while, letters or no letters. As it happens, she in the middle of washing her hair and does not wish to chat, which suits Cosmo fine.

The bike starts without difficulty and there is no black smoke now, and it behaves itself for the rest of the morning. He has left the letters for Babis till last. There is nothing nice about seeing that man! Babis may be younger than he is, but the lawyer's manner is intimidating and he uses long words that Cosmo does not understand. Tension builds in Cosmo whenever he talks to the man, and he feels that at any moment Babis is going to bully him, and this in turn makes him shrink and leaves him unable to speak. But he must steel himself to ask how probate is coming along. Five months he has been paying out for it, and so far he has seen no results.

'You needn't have knocked, just put them through the letterbox,' Babis says as he opens the door, his crisp white shirt untucked and a piece of toast in one hand. Jam has been spread liberally on the toast and it drips over the lawyer's fingers.

'I would have, only I just wondered how the probate was going.' Cosmo recalls how they used jam in a play at school once for blood. He stifles a snigger.

'I told you, you cannot rush these things, they take time. Talking of things taking time, is this all the post there is? I am expecting something. There's nothing left in your sack, or back at home, is there?'

'No!' It is the most Cosmo can manage, all mirth gone.

'Well, after seeing those letters to Maria ...' Babis pauses, his chin in the air, looking down his nose at Cosmo. 'I trust they were nothing important?'

He pauses again, taking a bite of the jam-laden toast. Cosmo can smell coffee boiling.

'But I was right to pay her a visit, it seems,' Babis concludes.

'What?' Cosmo feels a surge of adrenaline coursing through his veins, and a picture of the letters still sitting on his shelf looms clear in his mind. He tries to compose himself but he cannot release the tension that has sprung into his neck. He clenches at one hand with the other, twisting his fingers.

'Pay her a visit. It turns out that I was right – she doesn't have a will. And then things took a very curious turn.'

Babis talks as if everything is a joke, or at least it seems to amuse him. Cosmo cannot tell if what he is saying is real or a joke. The armpits of his shirt become wet. He should have just posted Babis's letters through the box. Nothing could be worse than Babis telling Maria that Cosmo is withholding her letters.

'You would be fascinated to hear who she has left all her worldly goods to, just fascinated.' Babis chews, his lips smacking.

Cosmo feels thrown. Isn't Babis talking about the letters now? It seems not. He needs to answer … What should his response be?

'Just fascinated to hear,' Babis repeats.

'Who?' Cosmo parrots.

'Ah, now that would be telling and, well, client confidentiality I'm afraid. I cannot possibly tell, but you would be fascinated to know. As I was!'

Babis nods his head sagely and then, having finished his toast, sucks the jam off his thumbs and fingers.

Is Babis trying to tease him or taunt him with his talk of letters and wills, or is this just the way he talks? It's hard to tell.

'What has whoever Maria makes her will out to got to do with me?' Cosmo says. It seems like a solid defence, a roundabout way of telling Babis he does not care to know about her business.

'Ah.' Babis wags his finger at him. 'It is a small village, every action we take makes only a small ripple at the start but sometimes these turn into waves that can spread to distant shores …'

Cosmo shifts from one foot to the other. He can sense that Babis is poking fun at him, but he cannot tell what the joke is.

'Well, I have a fence to fix,' he says.

He would like to say more about the probate, but he is desperate to get away now. It is uncomfortable listening to Babis talk about Maria, not just because he knows about the letter, but because – well, it just is.

He turns to leave, climbs on his bike and readies himself to kick the stand up, but his stomach is in knots. He needs to know what is being done about probate or he will just feel that Babis has played a trick on him, charging a monthly fee for nothing. He leaves the stand and dismounts from his bike.

'Oh, have you found that you had some more letters for me tucked away somewhere?' Babis puts his hand out to receive them.

'No. I want to know what you have done about probate.'

'I thought we talked about this already. Why the rush?'

'Because I am paying.' He can feel heat rising in his neck.

'I see. So you want a detailed account of current progress? That will cost extra.'

'I don't want any letter, I just want you to tell me. What exactly have you done?'

'So far?'

'How could it be anything else?'

It is Babis's turn to colour, just slightly, and Cosmo gains some confidence from this.

'I have conducted the title searches to ensure there is no charge against the land and you will be glad to know that there is not. There was still a last payment to be made on the fans but that cannot be dealt with until I have worked through things with your mama's accountant, to see what was owing at the point of death.'

Cosmo gulps. The last payment on the fans? He has never thought about how they were paid for, and if she owes taxes does he also become responsible for that? He has never been in debt in his life, apart from when he bought his bike, but the payments for that only lasted four months. He shouldn't have asked, he just shouldn't have asked.

'I bet you wish you hadn't asked now, don't you?' Babis smirks, and Cosmo bites his tongue.

To distract himself from the thought of probate and what it will cost, and because he wants to show Babis that he is conscientious, he conducts one last search of the various pockets in his bag for any envelopes he might have missed. Babis closes the door on him and Cosmo breathes a sigh of relief – just as he finds a letter he has missed. He hopes with all his heart that it is not for Babis. No – it is for Irini, Marina's daughter-in-law. He lets out an audible sigh of relief.

'*Malaka.*' Cosmo hisses the word quietly towards Babis's front door, kick-starts his bike and drives it very fast indeed for the few seconds it takes to cross the square to the corner shop.

He loves the shop, always has done, ever since Marina opened it when she was just twenty-nine. He knows how old she was because they are the same age. It felt at the time like their paths collided for a moment. Marina's husband had just died and his baba had just passed away. But whereas he has just plodded on in his same way all these years, Marina proved – and is still proving – that it is possible to grow wings following such an event. It gave him the hope to think that he too could change his life's path. With his baba gone, he had thought he could stop being the one who had to pacify his mama, maybe even move out. Those few glorious days when he thought life might be whatever he wanted it to be …

How quickly that dream had vanished when it was made clear that his mama was now his responsibility. How lucky she was, they said, her cronies at the church, to have a son to look after her, whilst others referred to him as 'poor Cosmo', who could never marry – not with the responsibility for his widowed mother on his shoulders.

So Marina and her shop became a symbol, an example of what might be possible. She was married off as a young girl to an old goat of a man twice her age, who provided nothing and took everything, and then left her widowed with two children and a pile of debt, yet here she was, turning the situation around and in doing so becoming the life and the very soul of the village with her corner shop. She is living proof to Cosmo that everything can change.

He trots up the step and is met by a blast of cool air from the unit over the door. Inside is in darkness, the light from the window obscured by promotional stickers and boxes of cotton reels, hairnets and paperclips piled on the ledge. The roof beams are hung with fly swats, beach balls in plastic net bags, mouse traps – both humane and the other kind. Cosmo does his best not to look at the latter. Since the episode with the fish, the thought of an animal in pain is more than he cares to entertain. The shelves overflow with tins and bottles and household necessities such as mop heads and dustpans. Brooms and shepherd's crooks lean in the corners. Sacks of rice, lentils, pasta and flour take up most of the floor space, but there is still a spare chair for any customer who wishes to stay for a chat.

'Hi, Cosmo.' Marina is behind the counter, which itself is stacked with biscuits, sweets, bubblegum and lighters standing sentinel in a cardboard display stand. Behind her, against the wall and reaching to the ceiling, are towers of cigarette packets, kept within easy reach. Sometimes it is Marina who serves, sometimes it is Irini. Petta, her son, helps out too, but since he has started to build a boat with his baba down by the jetty he spends little time in the shop.

'Hi, Marina.'

She puts her hand out for the letter and reads the address.

'Oh,' she says. 'Irini's in the back, or I can take it.'

'Marina?' The call comes from the narrow back door by the shelves where the bread is stacked, covered with a light nylon gauze net.

'Oh, hi, Cosmo.' Irini is silhouetted as she enters. 'Marina, do you want some food now?' she asks.

'Yes, sure, it's been quiet for the last hour. Cosmo, have you eaten?'

'Er, no.'

'Come on then. We haven't seen much of you since you got so busy with your oranges.'

Marina leads the way to the courtyard that divides the shop from the house, where a lemon tree dominates and the smell of roast tomatoes is only interrupted by the occasional whiff of the wisteria that trails over the courtyard walls.

Cosmo is repeating in his head what Marina just said – 'busy with his oranges'. In other words, not 'lazy'!

'Is Petta here?' Marina asks, and just as she speaks Petta strides out into the courtyard through a side door. Cosmo finds Petta's size a little intimidating, and he is always so powerfully jolly that Cosmo is often left wondering if there is a flip side to his nature, if there is equal force in all his moods. Not that he has ever heard any rumours to back this up. It might just be his own fears, as the size of the man does catapult him back into feeling like a small boy.

'Is Miltos with you?' Marina asks.

'No. Baba went to Juliet's for lunch.' Petta leans down to kiss them, first Irini on the mouth and then Marina on the forehead. Cosmo tries not to watch too intensely. He cannot ever remember kissing his mama on the forehead, or anywhere else for that matter, not since he was a child. But it is the kiss from Petta to Irini that lingers in his mind and causes him to feel unsettled.

'Little Angelos.' Marina opens her arms wide and squats down by the wooden table that is set with food. A toddler comes running from inside the house and throws himself into her arms.

Angelos then spots Cosmo and runs to him, and he squats just in time to catch the boy as he throws himself into a hug.

'Hello, little man,' Cosmo says, wondering if his nervousness shows. He does not have much contact with children and he is really not sure what to do with them. He also wonders if Petta will feel peeved that his son ran to this stranger, rather than to him first. But before his thoughts can take him any further, Angelos has prised himself away and is holding out a small red car …

'Oh, what have you got there? Now that is a fine car,' Cosmo says, feeling rather self-conscious.

But the little boy has lost interest and he runs to his baba, who bends down, scoops him up and lifts him high in the air.

'Come on then, let's eat,' he says, with Angelos held above his head as if he weighs nothing at all.

'But wait.' He stops and looks around. 'Where is my son?' Angelos giggles and squirms. 'Angelo? Where are you?' The child giggles and squirms even more.

'I can hear you,' says Petta, 'but I just can't see you ... Ah well, I will eat by myself then.' And the big man sits, the child still held high.

'I think you will find your son above your head,' Irini says, as if this game has been played a thousand times before. She begins to put food on the plates. With the door to the shop wide open, the courtyard catches a slight breeze and the leaves of the lemon tree flutter.

Petta looks up. 'Oh, there you are! Well, you come down here and sit next to me ... There you go.' And he carefully lowers Angelos into his high chair. 'So, how are you, Cosmo?'

'Oh, you know,' Cosmo says non-committally.

'Well, I'm sure it has been tough,' Petta says, and he offers the basket of bread.

Cosmo grunts his reply. He cannot put into words the mess of emotions that have been, and still are, swimming around inside him. They seem to change so quickly at the moment. It is hard to get a handle on how he truly feels about his mama. This family seems to genuinely enjoy each other's company as human beings, and by comparison his own family dinners were awkward, his baba always silent and giving the impression he was resenting every moment. His mama would press for her husband's attention, describing the trials of her morning – again – whilst he, Cosmo, sat silently, not quite understanding what was going on.

When he was very young, he did not realise that in fact they both wanted to avoid talking about certain things in his presence, but he would hear them hiss and snarl at each other after he was in bed, and these terse exchanges that he was not supposed to overhear somehow made him feel very unsure of his safety. As he got older, however, he realised that it had nothing to do with him.

Irini passes him a plate of stuffed tomatoes and wine is poured in his glass. It is a welcome change of fare. Not that he would ever say anything against Stella's chicken and lemon sauce, but for variety this is such a treat.

Petta dips his bread into the olive oil that has mixed with tomato juice in the bottom of the salad bowl in the centre of the table. Marina makes a noise as she chews. Angelos sits on Irini's knee, and she feeds him little bits of food that she has dipped in the juice on her own plate. She forks mouthfuls of food for herself in between feeding her son. No one says much – they enjoy the space, the food and the company without much chatter and the whole experience is very relaxed.

Just for a moment, about halfway through the meal, Cosmo is touched by sadness. He could have had this. If his mama had allowed him to get close to some girl in the village, maybe she would have taken him as a husband and this life could have been his. Maybe it would be his daughter in Irini's seat, with his grandchild on her knee.

After the plates are all cleared, Cosmo chats about Petta's boat and Marina and Irini talk about Angelos's morning as they drink a coffee. When Petta has drained his cup to the grounds at the bottom he suddenly seems anxious to be going.

'You understand, it needs to be waterproofed inside and out before any bad weather comes,' he tells Irini, speaking of his boat, with a kiss and a ruffle of Angelos's hair. Cosmo stands to shake the man's hand. Petta grins at him broadly and suggests he comes down to see the boat. Cosmo feels slightly less afraid of him but he is not sure he will go – maybe one time with Thanasis, perhaps. He assures Petta he will and the big man leaves.

Angelos starts to whinge, and Irini excuses herself and takes him inside, then comes back out and tells Marina that she is going to start on the stocktaking, before going into the shop.

Cosmo sits back and lets his stomach expand. Angelos begins to cry and Marina is quick to fetch him.

'You're not ready to sleep, are you, my little man?' she coos to the baby, and she sits back down opposite Cosmo.

'I never thought I would love again as I love this little man,' Marina says to Cosmo. 'How are you doing?'

She looks him straight in the eye and Cosmo squirms.

'It's hard, isn't it?' she says, and a little frown appears, knotting the skin between her eyes. 'If you love them, then there is nothing but pain. If the love was mixed with – well, other things, then it gets to be complicated.'

She takes a half breath. 'It is no secret that I didn't love Manolis. I didn't even *like* Manolis, but after he was gone it was like he was still here' – she looks around the courtyard – 'and I didn't dare do things in case he came back or rose from his grave or something.'

Cosmo smiles, but only because he is not sure what else to do.

'You smile, but I know you know what I am talking about. Your mama was not an easy woman.'

Cosmo feels the blood drain from his face.

'It was visible?' he asks.

'Were we not babies together, growing up together, seeing each other every day for the entirety of our lives?' she says. 'Besides, God bless her soul, it is not a secret that I never had any love for the woman. Not that I had strong feelings against her, as you know. It was just – well, not everyone suits everyone. Besides, once I was married to Manolis I saw who she was all the more clearly. But then I would, wouldn't I? I had another like her to judge up close!' A glazed look passes across her eyes.

Cosmo nods as if he has always thought so, but this is all coming as news to him.

'So, how are you?' Marina asks again. Angelos is playing with her necklace, an evil eye made of blue glass, on a gold chain.

He shrugs and tries to pin down one emotion … But he cannot speak its name – that would be terrible.

'Go on,' Marina says gently, 'I can assure you I had all your feelings and more when Manolis died. I thought I would burn in hell forever for some of my thoughts.'

'Well, I am beginning to think she did not suit me,' Cosmo says quietly. Saying these words gives him the same feeling as the time he swore by accident in church. 'Mostly what I feel is relief,' he adds, and all the blood that drained from his face rushes back and makes his cheeks feel hot.

'Oh yes, relief,' she says, as if she remembers the feeling only too well. This gives Cosmo courage.

'I thought I would miss her more, but as time goes on I feel this increased sense of ...' He stops to consider, to choose a word that fits. 'Freedom. Yes, freedom.' He thinks some more, before adding, 'And anger, I think.'

'And how much! I think I didn't dare to be angry with him when he was alive – I was too scared of him. But after he was gone, oh yes! Well, the shop is proof! So angry I opened his precious little *apothiki* to the world and sold off all that was his! Ha ha!'

Cosmo finds he is smiling with her, but the anger turns his mouth to a snarl.

'Yes, anger.' Saying the words feels easier this time.

'And of course – guilt,' Marina offers.

Cosmo focuses his attention inside his head, then his chest and then his stomach ... Oh yes, there it is, churning his lunch: guilt.

'Well, it was for the world to see that she suffocated you.' Marina kisses the baby's hand that is reaching to her face.

But Cosmo is left reeling. 'Suffocate' is a very daring word, but it feels like such a good fit, and all the time he just thought that was how all mamas were behind closed doors.

'Yes, she suffocated me, and I feel guilty that I am happy that she is gone.' The words feel like the bravest thing he has ever said and he worries that Marina will consider him to be a sinner.

'Well, take it from me, let go of that one first. You have no reason to feel guilty for anything. You gave up your life to look after that woman, a duty you could have turned your back on.'

'Not if I wanted to stay in the village,' Cosmo observes.

Marina nods in agreement and Angelos reaches for her earrings; he finds that his head is near her shoulder and rests it there, his eyelids flicking for a moment before closing.

'I'd better lay this one down,' she says.

'And I'd better go,' Cosmo responds. A part of him wants to stay. Marina makes talking easy – he feels like some of his sins have been forgiven and he feels lighter.

'Well, I am here,' she says by way of goodbye, and she invites him to come again, before standing and going into her house. Cosmo lets himself out by the side gate, noting on his way out that her wisteria needs watering. He hopes she notices too.

At home, the warmth of the day and his full stomach guide him to lie down on the daybed for a sleep. The sadness he felt during lunch is still there.

The orchard is fenced around the sides and at the back, where it borders Vangelis's olive grove. The fence, although a little rusty in places, is in good condition generally, and it is certainly not old enough to have been erected by Cosmo's baba. Oddly, the front of the orchard, on the road side, is open for its full length. Cosmo wonders if his mama fenced the back because of some dispute with Vangelis. That would fit. She often complained about him, for some reason or another. But last week he seemed friendly enough, leaning over from his side for a chat.

At the back, in the far corner, a hole has appeared in the wire, perhaps made by a dog, and Cosmo squats to examine it. In a way, it seems pointless to do anything about it, since the whole property is not secured and dogs can just wander in from the road if they want to, but seeing as he is responsible now Cosmo feels he should maintain it. The flexible wire he has brought with him will be perfect for the job.

The rusty metal seems to bite into his fingers, resisting his efforts as he pulls at it, coaxing the two sides back into position to try to close up the hole. The hole continues to gape, reluctant to close up, so he threads the wire back and forth, pulling on each return. Finally, he bends the wire this way and that to break it, and the heat it builds up burns his fingers.

'Oh, come on,' he mutters, and at last the wire becomes soft and breaks. 'Thank you,' he says.

It won't be dark for a few hours yet, and it would be a good time to get on with any other jobs around the orchard that need doing, but he seems to have done them all and so he wanders his way home.

As he approaches the church he can see Maria carrying her rubbish to the bins. She holds the bag at arm's length, and a procession of cats trail behind her. If he were closer he would be able to hear her talking to them, in the soft, sweet voice she used before the time of the rejection letter. A group of boys, brown-skinned and shirtless, pause in their game to let her pass, but as she turns back in the direction of her house, one of them kicks the ball across her path. They will be taunting her, Cosmo realises – thoughtlessly and without real malice, but to Maria it will feel so unkind.

They get a rise out of her, and so of course it is natural that they tease her. They stole her bicycle once and hid it in an orange grove. Maria blamed the papas, certain it was he who took the bike, and there was no telling her otherwise even when it was found and returned to her.

By the time he reaches the church she is back in her house, and Cosmo turns down his lane and slows his bike to a stop.

Poppy has left his clothes, pressed and neatly folded, on the kitchen table. He will have a shower and change. He feels sweaty and dusty.

The cold water runs over his face and down his back and feels very refreshing. The searing heat of August has lessened but the beginning of September can still be warm. Outside the bathroom window, the grapes hang from the pergola, plump, heavy and deep red.

'Ah, I can try to make wine with them this year!' he says out loud. 'No more of her damned cordial!'

He dries himself briskly with a small towel but the heat has already done most of the job. Naughtily, he wanders naked into the kitchen. It is not likely Poppy would drop round for anything at this time in the evening, and anyone else would knock, so he enjoys the feeling of the air on his skin and he takes his time to put on fresh clothes.

Inspecting the cuffs of his shirt, he wonders if he would be better off taking out the large stitches his mama put in. The colour of the cotton is wrong and it does not do a good job of hiding the frayed edges.

Petta won't have any such worries. Irini will sit and stitch his shirts, no doubt, or Marina. What must that be like, to not have to worry about these things? He could try to restitch them himself, but he doesn't even know where she kept the sewing box. Probably in her room. He has not been in there since the funeral, and it was not a place he can remember being invited to enter. At some point, of course, he will have to go in there and sort through her belongings. But not yet. He is not ready to face that yet.

He takes a pair of scissors from a nail on the edge of the kitchen shelf and cuts away the thread and then, very carefully, with his arm resting on the table, he trims the ragged edge of the cuff. Even by his standards, the shirt is fit for the bin. Of course, he agrees with his mama's frugal attitude, in principle at least. It is best to make do with what you have, and there is no point in throwing away things that are serviceable, then wasting money buying new.

But she was not consistent and that always bothered him. When was she ever frugal with the air conditioning? She would leave the television on all day from morning till night – and sometimes refuse to turn it off even then, saying the background noise soothed her. His last electricity bill was shockingly small compared to when she was alive.

Cosmo examines the result of his efforts. The cuff is not much better than it was, and the shirt is worn at the elbows too, and at the collar. *I will buy a new one*, he decides. *I will buy two!*

Chapter 13

The following day, in a shop in Saros he has never been to before, Cosmo looks at himself in the mirror and grins. With the shirt and trousers he is trying on, his clean-shaven face and his newly slender frame, he hardly recognises himself. He is not in the habit of looking in mirrors and, until now, if his reflection ever caught his eye in a shop window, it would reveal a short, hairy-faced man, scruffy and unkempt, with his stomach stuck out like a six-year-old's, his back arched to compensate for the weight. None of these traits is evident now, not one. He is no taller than he was, of course, but he doesn't appear so short because he is no longer so stout.

'They suit you.' The girl is looking at his new clothes in the mirror. He pulls himself up to his full height. If he gets a haircut as well, the villagers will not be able to recognise him.

'Can I wear them now?'

'Of course. I will take off the tag and wrap your old clothes.'

'If you would be so kind, could you just slip my old clothes into the bin? I think they have had their day.'

'Sure. This new look suits you much better. Those are a little old-fashioned.' She pushes his old clothes, which look like a pile of rags in this shiny environment, to one side on the counter, quickly removes the tags that dangle from his neck and waist and tells him that there is a sale on and everything is twenty per cent cheaper than marked.

'And I will give you a good price as well.' She discounts the clothes some more.

Why on earth has he not done this years ago? His mama so impressed upon him how expensive clothes were that he never thought to buy any. Then, once every few years, she would go into town and bring him back something from the *laiki* – the street market ... Not even from a shop, so how cheap would that have been?

'I think I'll take the other shirt too.' Cosmo hands her the first shirt he tried on. She wraps this, and puts it in a bag with a rope handle. He walks out with a smile and just a small swagger.

As he passes a barbershop, he falters and then tells himself he has no choice. There is no mama with her scissors now to cut his hair and the ends are well below his collar.

Haircuts were always such an ordeal, to be avoided for as long as possible and endured when the inevitable time arrived. Her scissors were invariably a hazard, and Cosmo can remember being made to sit, from a young age, on a stool in the kitchen – stock-still for fear of the scissors that flashed and clicked angrily away around his ears. His baba underwent the same treatment, and he never questioned it; it was just the way haircuts were administered.

Once she did indeed snip a piece out of his baba's earlobe – and how it had bled! There was no sympathy. A dishcloth was shoved in his hand so he could stem the flow of blood, and she started work on the other side.

Of course, the whole procedure was not reciprocal. Mama went to the hairdresser in Saros every month or so. She would complain when the prices went up but no one ever suggested that he or his baba cut her hair.

He clenches his teeth at the memory. No matter how hard he tried, he could not keep his head still enough, and she would yank it back to the correct position, tutting and snorting with impatience.

Afterwards, with his neck and shoulders itching, his baba would ruffle his newly shaved hair and give him a conspiratorial nod, but only when she wasn't looking.

Of course, in his teens he tried to let his hair grow as long as possible, but eventually he gave in, as different sections seemed to grow at different rates and he had to put up with her complaining that he was reflecting badly on her with his scruffy look. To this last his baba agreed, and finally it was easier just to do as she said.

The barbershop is an alien place – all mirrors and chrome. He hasn't completely made the decision when someone with a neat haircut comes out, swinging the door wide, and another man in a white shirt, comb in hand, greets Cosmo with such warmth it feels rude to walk away. The man chats about politics and football, and gives him a haircut that makes him look ten years younger in less than ten minutes.

'That's a good exchange,' Cosmo quips, but the barber doesn't seem to understand.

In all, it is a very pleasant experience, with no one squawking at him to sit still, sit up, turn his head, lean forward or obey any of the other hundred commands his mama issued as she hacked away at his scalp. The cut hair is brushed from his neck and from under his chin to stop it making its way down his shirt and itching for days. The barber wishes him 'go to the good' and hopes he will see him again soon.

'I mean, how do you mistake an earlobe for hair?' he says as he hops onto his motorbike. It is refreshingly cool around his ears on the ride back to the village.

Eager to show everyone his new look, he decides to have an early lunch at Stella's.

'Hello, sir, are you new around here, how can I help you?' Mitsos quips as he walks in.

Stella looks up from behind the counter where she is cutting chips.

'Oh my, look at you,' she says, leaving the chips and coming around the counter to look him up and down. 'Are you going to a wedding?'

'No, just thought it was time.'

'You'll be turning a few heads in the village walking around like that. I noticed you'd lost a few kilos but …' She whistles.

'He'll be looking for a wife now his mama's gone.' Mitsos winks at him. His words carry a certain weight – after all, he married Stella very late in life, and they make Cosmo think – just for a second, before he dismisses the idea. Mitsos has charm, and it is different.

'Yes, indeed, Cosmo, and a woman would be very proud to have a man like you,' Stella says. Cosmo is surprised at her teasing but when he looks at her face there is no trace of humour there. She seems serious.

'You think?' Cosmo looks down at himself, at his new clothes, trying to see what they see.

'Yes.' Stella is firm and Mitsos nods. He takes three glasses and puts some coffee and sugar in each.

'It's a nice thought,' Cosmo says quietly, and he leans towards Stella as Mitsos uses the electric mixer to make the drinks. 'But,' Cosmo whispers, close to her ear. 'I know I am a bit slow.'

She leans towards him and whispers back, 'Slow, fast – what does this have to do with you being a decent human?'

'No, at school – they made fun of me because I was slow.' He glances at Mitsos, but he is absorbed in his noisy job.

'We are all slow in some directions and fast in others,' says Stella. He frowns. 'You might be slow at maths or whatever, but you are observant of people, and quick to understand their emotions.'

Cosmo pulls away from her slightly so he can focus on her face. Her dark, shoulder-length hair glistens in the streak of sunlight coming through the door and she smells of freshly cut potatoes. Her neat features are composed, and she looks sincere.

'And slow to know your own good points.' Now she laughs and pulls away, leaning towards Mitsos, who has finished making the coffees.

Mitsos turns the chicken on the grill and the three go outside and sit around a table, their chairs pushed back, legs outstretched.

'So, how are the oranges?' says Mitsos. Stella turns her head, following a sound of bells, which are dully clanking, and she listens as the noise gets louder; presently the staccato castanet of a hundred hoofs drums on the road as a herd of goats enter the village and begin their dash up the main street. Cosmo has heard the sound so many times he does not bother to turn. Across the road, in the square, Vasso comes out of her kiosk to push her magazine rack under the awning in preparation for the onslaught. Cosmo watches her drag empty beer crates from the back of the kiosk and place them at intervals around her domain to dissuade the animals.

'Whose goats are these?' Stella says. Cosmo now turns his head and then shifts his chair so he can watch the flood of animals coming up the road. When the lead goat sees them it falters, alert, and only moves again as those behind push it forward. Many of them have bells around their necks, each striking a different note, and the music they make is a free, happy sound that makes Cosmo wish he was up in the hills, free of civilisation, alone with nature. Judging by the look on Mitsos's face, it has a similar effect on him.

'I think they belong to Nicolaos, the Australian,' he says.

'I had a letter addressed to him the other day as "Nicolaos the Australian",' Cosmo says, and they all chuckle. 'There is "Nicolaos the Australian", "Nicolaos the Canadian" and another Nicolaos who is simply known as "Sugar", because he is diabetic.'

The first goats leave a space around the eatery tables, but as more and more come the distance decreases until the animals are bumping into table legs and a chair is knocked over. Behind the herd run two dogs, and way behind the dogs, walking at a very steady pace, is Nicolaos himself. Across the road, Vasso is waving at the herd with a folded newspaper and shouting at them to move away.

'*Kalimera.*' Nicolaos stops by the eatery, wiping his brow with the back of his forearm. He rests both hands on top of his crook and looks at each of them in turn, his gaze lingering on Cosmo.

'How are they?' Mitsos asks, nodding in the direction of the herd, which has turned up the road that runs along the top of the square, still followed by the dogs. The clanking and clonking of the bells quietens, and Vasso pulls her magazine rack back out from under her awning.

'All fine. Business good?'

'*Etsi ketsi* – so-so,' says Stella. 'You want a glass of water?'

'Thanks,' says Nicolaos. 'Business will pick up when we lose this heat. Then the whole village will be rushing to you for a hot meal.'

'True enough, we cannot complain,' Mitsos replies, and, with this, Nicolaos drinks deeply from the glass Stella has brought him. Then he releases his crook, lifts it with one hand and slides it across his shoulders, one wrist hooked over each end so his hands dangle as he strides away.

'I don't think he recognised you,' Stella says and starts to giggle.

'That's a point – he didn't speak to you at all. I also wondered why he stopped ... He wanted to see who you were!' Mitsos says.

'Nah, don't be silly. I deliver his letters at least once a month. Not that he is ever in,' Cosmo says.

'Seriously, he had no idea who you were!' Stella is giggling and has had to put her frappe down to avoid spilling it. She wipes the front of her floral-print dress with her hand.

Cosmo rather likes this idea. He is a new man – hopefully a new and improved man. Quite out of the blue, this makes him think of Maria. Maybe she will see him differently too? Naturally, her letters, which are still sitting on the shelf in his kitchen, also come to mind. They annoy him. Who is this anonymous letter writer anyway, and why should he have precedence over Cosmo in telling Maria his feelings?

Then another thought comes to him and he wonders why he has never had it before: he could try to find out who this anonymous letter writer is. If this man wants to woo Maria, then he should get on with it, and if not he should back off, give someone else a chance. Of course, it is not really Cosmo's place to interfere, but it is for Maria's sake too. If whoever it is turns out to be a good man – well, then, so be it, he will deliver the letters and stand aside. But if he is not a good man, if he is just toying and playing, writing when he is drunk or when his mama or someone has scolded him, then to hell with him – burn the letters and confess his own love to Maria.

'Are you all right?' Stella pats him on the back, and he holds his frappe tightly. The wanderings of his mind have taken his breath from him.

He revises his last thought immediately. He will send no man to hell, even if it is just a saying. But maybe the letters could meet with an accident? Accidents do happen. But if the anonymous lover is a better man than he, Cosmo, is, then Maria deserves that, and he could mastermind a way to get them together. Yes, that is a plan.

The idea seems both empowering and terrifying.

'You all right? You're all red.' Stella's hand is still on his back.

'Fine, just went down the wrong way.' He feels exposed with these thoughts rushing through his mind, in such close proximity to his friends. He sips the last of his frappe, offers to pay. Stella pulls a face and Mitsos smiles.

'Well, I'd better get on,' Cosmo says vaguely, and he stands to walk off in his usual way – flat-footed, slouching, stomach out. But the stiffness of his new clothes pulls at him, and he stands taller. His first stride is longer and slower than usual, his stomach held in and his head erect. It feels good. It also feels good to be away where he can think more clearly. He needs one of the letters in his hand to know what to do next.

Back at home, he shuts the door with a bit more of a bang than he intended. He takes one of the letters and sits in his mama's chair, with its age-worn arms, at the end of the kitchen table. He expects inspiration to come, that his new clothes will have an effect on his thinking, but after half an hour of staring at the handwriting he is no closer to knowing what to do and he slopes off to bed, a grey cloud fogging his mind, convincing him that no matter what clothes he wears or how much time passes his life is never going to change.

Chapter 14

The Christmas decorations displayed on Marina's counter appear to be the same ones she had last year – and the year before that, no doubt – and they serve to remind Cosmo that the days have become months and he has still not worked out how he will find out who has written the letters.

'Do you want a snowman?' Marina says.

It has been a long, hard day for Cosmo. After his rounds, he had to mend the back fence again. Grigoris, who was working on his own fence in the next orchard, told him that the gypsies cut holes in the fences so they can harvest a crate or two of oranges whenever they choose, a couple from each orchard, and sell them cheap to the stallholders at the *laiki*. That was his mama's way of thinking too, to blame the gypsies, but the fences are old, and there's bound to be a place where they are weakest. Surely it could be age, or a dog, just as easily? But Grigoris clicked his tongue and rolled his eyes when Cosmo suggested this.

It took Cosmo a couple of hours to pull the fence together and weave new wire to hold it. It was more strenuous work than he expected and he is tired now.

'A snowman – when do we ever have snow?' he asks, with a frown of surprise.

'Ach,' Marina says, 'they were sent by some company in Athens. A promotion.' She picks up one of the snowmen and peers at it for a moment, then puts it down again on the counter.

'I'll stick to the traditional New Year festivities, thank you, Marina,' he says.

She looks at the snowman's cartoon-like face and smiles before putting it down.

'A small bottle of Plomari, please.' Cosmo takes out his money, thanks Marina kindly and feels very pleased to be going home. A nip of ouzo and then maybe he will be recovered enough to go for some supper at Stella's. No, a *meze* will do at the *kafenio*. Or perhaps Stella's would be nice … He will decide after his ouzo.

At home, he flops onto a kitchen chair and, with a sigh, he stands again to get a glass. He has moved all the canisters from the shelf and given them to Poppy, who was very pleased with them. She said they were from the fifties, possibly Italian. Cosmo could easily believe they were that old, if not more. They had been there ever since he could remember and he was glad to see the back of them. The coffee is still kept on the shelf, but in the foil packet now, and the rest of the shelf he uses for glasses and cups. But he might eventually pare them down; after all, he only uses one at a time and it is simple enough to rinse them. Behind the glasses, propped against the wall, are the letters to Maria. Once every few days he takes the time to think how he can find the writer.

He scowls at the envelope, and at the wall, which is still the same putrid light green. The sight of the letters depresses him. 'Come on, apply yourself,' he mutters, and he tosses the letters on the table, then cracks open the ouzo bottle and pours himself a good measure.

'Just do it, just think about it until something comes to mind ... Stella says I am good at people – well, the writer is a person, so think, think!' He knocks back the first glass in one and pours another, wincing at the burn in his throat but enjoying the sensation of his muscles relaxing.

He traces the coffee mark on the first envelope and the lines where it has become creased in his pocket. The coffee spots look like eyes, the crease a smile.

The observation provokes a light laugh, and it lifts his spirits.

'So you are alive, are you? Well, I am good with people so what do I know about you, eh?'

He examines the handwritten address again.

'Nothing,' he answers himself, but then his eyes widen and he rubs his chin and laughs again. 'But I know who it is not! Yes, that is how to start.' He jumps up and takes paper and pen from his satchel and sits again.

'People you are not ...' He speaks as he writes. 'Grigoris,' he begins, and then adds to himself, 'Because he cannot write – and nor can old Stamatis.'

He goes on writing, adding to the list of names until he has included all the men in the village he has had to read letters to, or who have asked him for help in composing a reply. He mouths the names under his breath as he writes.

When he has finished, he scans the list, which contains a good twenty-three names. Names of people he is unofficially responsible for, in a way, and who rely on him to help conduct their affairs, both formal and private.

'That's quite a job.' He whistles through his teeth. The injection of vitality the alcohol sends through his body makes the ouzo bottle call out to him, and he takes another gulp.

'Now what? What else do I know? The person can write – that is clear, of course, and proved by all the letters, over the years.'

'Ah yes, so, his age. He must be, well ...' He cannot imagine whoever it is being much younger than Maria. More likely, he is a little older. He cannot think of a couple where that is not the case. Maybe in Athens or somewhere like that, but not here in the village. Often there is five, ten, even fifteen years' difference.

The handwriting confirms this. It has not changed significantly, which suggests that the first letters were not sent by a love-struck boy but by someone who was already a man. Maria was around twenty when the rejection letter came and the anonymous lover's first letter came about a year after that. So the person must be fifty or more.

'Ha! The net is closing, my friend.' He laughs, but the merriment dies in his throat.

He taps his pen on the sheet of paper. He could make a list of every single man in the village over fifty who does not need him to write their letters. He turns over to a clean sheet in the notebook. For a moment this brightens his outlook – that list will not be very long. But then with a heavy sigh it occurs to him that whoever it is will not necessarily be a single man. He hopes he is, though, or else this anonymous lover has been playing a very unfair game. If that turns out to be the case, the letters he has recently sent are definitely going to meet with an accident.

He taps his lips with the pen. He has a feeling there is something else that would help narrow down this list before he begins to write, but no inspiration comes.

'What else do I know about him? Male, over fifty, can write. And the postmark shows he is local. But maybe he is from Saros!' This thought deflates him and he puts down the pen.

But wait! He looks up and out of the small window by the front door. 'I remember he said he saw her at the church at Easter one year, and at a wedding.'

Now, whose wedding was that? Petta and Irini's? Yes, there have been no others for ages! Well, there was no one from outside the village around that day, not even any of the farmers from high in the hills who only ever seem to come down on such occasions. Oh yes, he is onto something and – hang on, didn't he also say he saw her going into Marina's shop on one occasion?

'I believe he did.' He rubs his chin. This really does sound like a local man, a man around the village.

'Panayia!' He swears as his nemesis suddenly becomes real to him. 'It could be someone I know, someone I meet every day!' A cold chill runs down his back and he stands to open the door to let some of the day's heat into the thick-walled stone cottage. He looks down the lane and across to the papas's house.

'Well, that is one person I can rule out,' he mutters to himself. There have been three priests presiding over the church in the village in the last few years. He smirks.

A man he recognises by his bouncing gait walks past the end of his road. Cosmo raises his hand in acknowledgement to Theo, who waves in return and disappears out of sight, only to reappear again a moment later.

'Cosmo, did a parcel come for me?' Theo calls.

'You will get a slip if it does,' Cosmo replies.

Theo waves and goes on his way.

Twisting on his heel, Cosmo returns indoors. Theo was just being impatient. He knows he will get a slip so he can pick it up in Saros. Although, there have been one or two occasions when Theo hasn't been able to close the *kafenio* and has asked Cosmo to sign for him at the depot in Saros. Cosmo has done that for a few people; he did it once for Stamatis when he had a twisted ankle, and he has done it for Marina, just because she asked. But mostly the villagers sign for and collect their own packages.

Something is stirring in his mind, a little bright light is blinking, and he can feel an idea forming, pulling itself to the surface He is ready to grasp hold of it, if only he can catch it before other thoughts cover it over.

'Oh!' Cosmo reacts as the idea slips into focus. His eyes open wide at his own genius.

'Could I? Could I do that and get away with it?' he marvels. 'If I had a form from the post office, who would not sign? I could get a sample of absolutely everybody's handwriting. What could I say it was for? ... A receipt for a letter, or to confirm I have delivered the post.

No, that sounds bad for me ... A petition for something, but then they might not agree with it. A petition to make me postmaster. Ha ha!'

Cosmo opens the ouzo bottle again, with a resounding pop of the cork. He doesn't drink often – or not very often, not every day, just when he is sad, or at happy moments.

This is a joyful moment.

'Now, what could I say?' he mumbles. He could pretend there is a parcel in Saros and say that if they sign he will bring it to them. He turns the glass. But if there is no parcel, he'll have to explain why ... Which is fine if he does this just the once, but he will have to do it many times and these men will sit in the *kafenio*, it will come up in conversation, they will compare notes. No, that will not do; they will realise there is something amiss. Hmm, it's harder than he thought.

Identity theft? That's a good one! It could be an EU directive that everyone's signature must be on record to prevent identity theft. A giggle starts in the back of his throat. It sounds just like something the government would do. But the government would want a signature from every single person in the village, and that would be a huge task. Something that big is bound to get back to the postmaster in Saros. No, it has to be something smaller. Something local.

He slugs back the last of the ouzo and pours another one. He knows from experience that the energy it is bringing him won't last long; all too quickly it will change, turn into a sluggishness, and he will feel incapable of moving. He would never drink this much in the *kafenio* – too many eyes. And until his mama died he could never have drunk at home. She would not have tolerated it; after all, she didn't want her son to die of a pickled liver, as her husband had.

So the feeling is still novel, and it is accompanied by a rebellious element. But when he is this drunk, some of her words do ring in his ears.

'It's hereditary,' she would say in an accusatory tone if she thought she could smell alcohol on him.

These assertions made him look twice at her. It wasn't so much that nothing he did could pass by unnoticed, uncommented on, which always kept him on his guard: it was the fact that even after the old man was gone she was still maintaining the pretence.

He had an idea who his real baba was. Poppy had let something slip once, but when he pushed, she clammed up.

Then there was another time, a bit later than that first event, when something else was said. Cosmo seems to remember it was a cold winter's day, and that the wind was blowing the leaves in circles around the corners of the village square. It must have been some years ago, because this was before the days of parcel slips and he had a heavy delivery for Poppy. Obviously he delivered it first – there was no point in lugging it around the village. He pulled up at his own back door with the idea of dropping the parcel and then having a coffee whilst he sorted the day's letters. What was it in Poppy's window that had changed from the day before? A change to the window display wasn't a common occurrence so it warranted comment.

'Looks good, Poppy.' He climbed from his bike and gestured at the clothes on the mannequin in the window. 'Did you get them locally?'

'A genuine nineteen sixty-one Anna Heropoiita. I got it more locally than you could guess,' Poppy chuckled.

'What's so funny?' he asked.

'You don't recognise it?'

She paused for a second but Cosmo must have looked blank because she continued, 'It was your mama's, and she just gave it to me.' Poppy was seated in her old chair on her doorstep, knitting, despite the cold.

He stared in astonishment at the pencil-skirted dress, the nipped-in waist and the red belt on the mannequin.

'It's hard to imagine one's parents having their own lives, isn't it?' Poppy was doing her best to stifle her smile as she watched his face with amusement. 'She said she had it bought for her. She's told you about her month in Athens, I presume, just before she married your baba?'

She had not, and Cosmo was quick to realise that if he said she had not then Poppy would seal her lips tighter than an octopus's beak. Even though his head was shaking 'no', he forced himself to say, 'We talk a lot,' which was not true either. Mama talked a lot, there was no denying that, but without inviting a response from Cosmo. Putting it this way to Poppy felt like less of a lie, though, somehow.

'Well, did she tell you it was her boss who bought it for her? I think he was sweet on her, don't you? I always suspected he was the reason she came back. I think he pressed her, wanted more than just to buy her dresses.' And she chuckled until she dropped a stitch and then started counting loops to herself to find her place again.

He went indoors and asked his mama straight.

'You never said you went to Athens for work. What made you come back?' he asked, the moment he was inside so he wouldn't lose his nerve.

'Who have you been talking to?' It was the look in her eyes that gave away her secret.

He could almost feel her fear. It was odd to see his sudden power reflected there, and there was a side of him that wanted to keep her there, just to experience the new position.

'You came back because your boss got sweet on you?' As he said the words, his intention wasn't to be mean – it was meant as a little tease, to keep the whole exchange a little light-hearted, perhaps, if she would allow it. He would have liked their relationship to be more like that. But he knew he also wanted to see that look on her face, that fear he was creating, a little longer.

'He was nobody. Nothing happened. Who has been telling you this nonsense?' she snapped, and the fear turned to anger, and that was it.

That was what told him this man from Athens was his baba. She had always maintained he was a premature baby. She had even implied that this was why he was slow. But the truth, he had suspected, was that she had been pregnant when she got married, and not even by her husband!

His mama never allowed him to speak about it again, and Poppy hardly spoke to him at all for a while, which only further confirmed that he was right. He had betrayed her trust. But surely he had a right to know who his baba was?

The first few days afterwards were so difficult. It was all he could think about. The questions, the accusations, just tumbled one on top of another through his mind like waves of torture. Each new question felt like the paramount route of enquiry. Who was his real baba? Why did his baba marry his mama if he knew she was pregnant? Did he even know? Should he try to find his real baba? Is he like him at all?

Then darker thoughts came. If he was abandoned once, by his baba, would he be abandoned again? This, he knew, was ridiculous. He was a grown man and the baba he grew up with was dead. It was most unlikely that his mama would abandon him now, especially now she needed him. But he recognised that he had become difficult to live with. He purposefully did the things that annoyed her the most. But the more he pushed her, the more she seemed to back down, and eventually he withdrew, said little, using his room at home just to sleep in as he spent more and more time at the *kafenio* and on his boat.

After living like this for a while, he felt as if he put on an act when he did see his mama. He was trying to be the person he was before he knew the secret. She didn't seem to notice the difference but he felt it, felt false with her, living a lie and lying to her like she had lied to him all his life.

Then something odd happened – or rather, it wasn't that something happened so much as he became aware of what he was doing. He was looking at faces. Not in the village, but when he went into Saros, especially around the bus station when buses came in from Athens. He would scan people's eyes, noses, mouths. After all, one of them could be his real baba, and any one of the younger people could be his brother or sister. He became obsessed with seeing himself in other people. At one point, there was a need for one of the postal workers to go all the way to Corinth for something, and when everyone else shied away from the task he was quick to volunteer. For the duration of the journey up there on the bus, he studied the people in their cars on the motorway. Once in Corinth, at the bus station by the canal, he found he could hardly get himself to leave. Any one of these people could be a blood relation – they could tell him who he was, be a piece of his puzzle. But he never saw a face like his own, and soon after the trip to Corinth he began to go for walks, talking to his real baba as if he walked by his side. They discussed why he did not marry his mum – she didn't want to – and how life would have been if they had been in touch as he grew up – much better, because he would have felt loved, like he belonged, important.

This phase seemed to last a while and he felt himself resenting his mama for forcing his real baba away. Then he began to worry that she was feeling rejected, and after a time the imagined conversations stopped and he returned to being the devoted, observant son, and she found her dominance again and they were back where they started. This made him wonder if his real baba was slow – stupid, even – which would explain why his mama treated him as she did and why he was seen as 'different' at school. Round and round these thoughts would go, torturing him.

So he stopped thinking. He took a look in the mirror, and as he stared he realised that his baba's identity made absolutely no difference to his life or to who he was. The man who counted was the one staring back at him in the mirror, and that was not going to change, no matter who his baba was. After a while – a year or two, maybe – he thought no more about it, telling himself that one day, perhaps after his mama was dead and would not be hurt, he might go and seek his real baba. One day.

He fills his glass again.
'Thanasis's name day!' he says suddenly. 'That's it! January, not even a full month away. I will get him a card, get everyone over fifty to sign it. It fits! Those who are his friends will do it, and those who say they are not that close I will just encourage them to sign anyway! "Where's the harm?" I will say! Brilliant!'

And with this thought he gulps back the rest of the ouzo in his glass and notices that the energy he had in his limbs is quickly turning to lethargy. He missed his window of opportunity to do some job or other around the house, but what the heck! He has come up with such a brilliant idea.

He grabs the bottle to pour himself his last drink before bed. It is very early to go to sleep and he has had no supper, but he can go to bed when he likes now, sleep as long as he wants, eat when he wants, drink when he wants. Besides, it is Sunday tomorrow. There is church, of course, and he should really try to make it. He has not been since the six-month remembrance service last month, but he has a choice in that too now!

'Ach!' He makes the guttural sound when he discovers the ouzo bottle is empty.

'Gamoto!' he swears, and he laughs because he has sworn and because he can swear, then puts the bottle in the sink, smooths his shirt front down. It is another new one. He bought it yesterday, and he derives a certain pleasure from carefully unbuttoning it, peeling it off, then folding it oh-so carefully and putting it on the back of the kitchen chair. As he stands to stagger his way to bed, it promptly falls on the floor.

Chapter 15

The television sits in a corner of the kitchen: a small portable thing with an aerial on top. How many times has he watched her fiddling with that aerial, moving it this way and that to get a better signal, or even getting him to take it outside, shouting, 'There! Leave it there.'

'How can I leave it here, Mama, when I am halfway across the road with my arm in the air?'

'Don't move … Oh, it's gone again now.'

For some reason the aerial has needed no wiggling since he turned the set on and tuned it in. What has been broadcast has been nothing but nonsense so far, but he is not actually watching it; he has only put it on for company. Families have been coming together for New Year all around the village. Previously, he celebrated New Year's Eve with Mama and Poppy. Poppy plays a mean hand of cards and she has the stamina to play past midnight and well into the early hours. His mama would stay up as late as she could, pouring drinks, filling bowls with crisps, betting on who would win or lose each hand until she finally fell asleep in her chair, her mouth open, snoring gently. Finally, when Cosmo started yawning too, Poppy would gather her winnings, wish him a Happy New Year and sneak out of the back door.

Last night, he stepped into the street to see the fireworks he could hear cracking over the village, but the houses either side of the narrow lane obscured his view of the sky and he saw next to nothing. He would have seen more from the square, but he found he wasn't in a state of mind where he wished to see people, so he went back inside and opened the ouzo bottle. That was company enough, and by around twelve-thirty he was snoring.

This morning it was a relief to wake up on New Year's Day feeling quite refreshed and not a bit hungover. The new year holds promise for the future, but there is a heaviness in his heart, and he cannot remember where it stems from. Slowly it creeps up on him, a realisation of what he had not really forgotten: he is alone. The air is not enriched with the enticing smells of fennel and garlic, roasting onions and tomatoes from the kitchen. He will not sit at lunchtime with Mama and Poppy as they gorge themselves on a feast fit for a King. Last year, Poppy had him bring an extra table over from her house because there was not enough room on the kitchen table for all the dishes the women had prepared.

The weather would always be mild, often sunny, and they would spend all afternoon on New Year's Day itself and into the evening sitting around that table.

He can still recall his baba dragging the table from by the back door to the middle of the narrow lane that ran behind their house and in front of Poppy's shop.

'No point in being squashed up,' his baba had said.

Poppy, who was sitting outside her emporium knitting as usual, pointed out that it wasn't as if anyone ever drove down the road anyway.

'Cosmo, bring Poppy's table too,' his baba said, a hand briefly ruffling Cosmo's hair. What a feeling that was – it brought a grin as wide as his cheeks would stretch, and even though he knew he was not big enough or strong enough to manhandle the folding table from behind Poppy's shop door, he went with the intention of doing it by himself anyway. How he struggled, careful not to put a corner or a leg into the glass door in his efforts, until his baba joined him and with a single arm lifted the table free of its confines and then left Cosmo to do the rest. It was heavy but he managed.

Both tables were piled high with dishes cooked by his mama and Poppy, and Baba had to bring out the glass-topped table from the best room, and his mama fussed that it would get broken. No harm came to the table, of course, and after her third glass of wine she declared it was very useful, and for a few years this was the model for their New Year street party.

It was probably the only day of the year that his mama allowed herself to drink, and what a difference it made. Her face would relax, her eyes would shine, her tongue would uncurl, and consequently her words became softer. In response, Baba would exhale, his shoulders would drop, he would put his feet up (but not on the glass table – that would have been a step too far) and they would banter, back and forth, and Poppy would stay silent and look from one to the other and smile, and it was possible to see why his parents had married each other in the first place. Whilst everyone was in this mood, even Cosmo was allowed a glass or two of wine, Poppy discreetly topping it up again and again until he would laugh along with his parents even if he had no idea what the joke was.

In all, it was the nicest day of the year. He felt as if they were family. They were together, and he was included, as were passers-by, of whom there were many at one time. Villagers, farming friends of Baba, on their way to relatives' houses were never allowed to go on their way without at least a drink. Women his mama knew took a detour to wish them all well.

Although, some of his mama's friends didn't stop. Even though their husbands were polite and ready to laugh as they talked to his baba, the men's hands remained in their pockets, jiggling keys and coins, indicating their wish to move on. Cosmo found these moments fascinating – the men in these couples dominating without having to say a word, the women obliging – and such a contrast to his own family; it would set him wondering whether he would be the dominant one if (or rather, back then when he still had hope, when) he found a wife? Or would he end up spending as much time as his baba did in amongst the orange trees from dawn till dusk? At that age, even that seemed romantic, one of the mysteries of adulthood.

New Year was only one day in the calendar but how he would have liked the rest of the year to be that way too. Not even name days or birthdays could compare.

There was a time when even friends from the *kafenio* would drop by: Mitsos, and Damianos, before he moved to America. Theo always passed by, every year, right up to the time he went to Athens and came back in love. Now, on the rare occasions his *kafenio* is closed, he is never seen. Every precious moment out of the *kafenio* is spent with his Tassia in their olive groves.

Mitsos doesn't come any more either, not since he married Stella. Baba's farmer friends long ago stopped using this street to get to where they need to go and his mama's friends dwindled in number over the years. Last year, and the year before – in fact, for a good ten years at least – it has been just his mama, himself and

Poppy. But it has still been pleasant enough. Joy was not something Mama seemed to be naturally imbued with, although Poppy – thank goodness for Poppy – made an effort to keep her smiling.

But there is no Mama this year, and Poppy informed him a few days ago, looking slightly embarrassed, that she was off to visit relatives. She would be taking a taxi to Saros and a train from there, and would he go in and water the plants whilst she was away?

They won't need watering yet. Tomorrow will do, but he has nothing else to do today, and with the *kafenio* closed he decides he will find out where all the plants are and locate the watering can so that when they do need watering it will be a simple and quick job.

The large iron key has a piece of red string tied around the shaft. To distinguish it, Poppy said. But the size and weight of it alone means it could not be mistaken. The smell of mothballs, old women and gossip greet him as he opens the door to her emporium. He has not been inside very often, despite living just across the street. Last New Year he went in to get the extra table, and then returned it a couple of days later, but he cannot remember ever stopping to look around.

As he does so now, his first impression is that the shop is smaller than he thought. The room is stuffed with things he cannot imagine anyone wanting. Racks of cheesecloth blouses yellowing along the creases, boxes of vests and T-shirts in a variety of colours. Who in the village is going to buy them? There are deflated beach balls in yellowing plastic packets, mop heads for a type of mop he has never seen, with faded labels. A box of knitting needles of assorted size, length and colour, some with round heads, others flat, some with points either end, and not a pair amongst them. Clothes, bedspreads and, he sees on inspection, curtains are piled on the floor, leaving just a narrow path down the middle of the shop. An old-fashioned diving suit dominates the space just in front of the counter and off to the left. It is complete with a spherical copper helmet, a circular window at the front, and the air tanks, which are on the floor next to it. He touches it gingerly, worried it might fall over. He has an urge to try it on, but as he moves to examine it from the side he stumbles over a pair of roller skates. He is tempted to put them on too but they are obviously much too small for him.

The counter, in the dark depths of the shop, is wooden, very dark and polished on a regular basis, with a glass top. The front of it houses drawers stuffed with long gloves, pieces of lace, a mess of jewellery, and a collection of worn leather belts, their chrome, peeling buckles facing front. On top of the counter is a box, inside which are cards for every occasion. The label on the box reads *Stack vertically*. Somewhat overwhelmed by the mountains of paraphernalia, Cosmo scans the room for plants. There are none in evidence; perhaps they are through the door by the makeshift dressing room, which is no more than the back corner of the shop, guarded by two mannequins whose fingers touch, a swathe of material draped over their arms to preserve the customers' modesty.

The door creaks and the smell of mothballs is replaced with something that could be tuna. A short corridor leads to a second door that opens into a tiny kitchen. There is a small wooden table, one wooden chair with fancy spindles, and a sink set in the wall. There is no stove and no fridge. On a shelf there is one small pan, one plate, one glass. On the kitchen table is a single-burner gas stove, its umbilical cord reaching to a small gas canister on the floor. The walls have discoloured with age and in some places the lean-to roof, of corrugated plastic, has let water in, streaking the walls. Even at this time of year, and relatively early in the day, the sun glares through the transparent roofing, heating the room to an uncomfortable temperature. The still air smells of age and dishwater. It must be like an oven in the summer. There are no plants here either.

On the far side of the table a door opens into an enclosed courtyard that is no bigger than the kitchen. The courtyard is a forest of green and in the middle is a single chair.

'So that's where you sit when your shop is closed,' says Cosmo, looking around him in wonderment at the mass of greenery. The air is cool and fresh in the courtyard, and the sun's rays are diffused by the foliage. Insects buzz and hum. He sits on the chair, closes his eyes and drifts for a moment. Yes, it is a very pleasant space, but somehow he feels uncomfortable, as if he is trespassing, and he makes his way back through the kitchen.

As he makes his way around the table towards the shop, his eye is caught by three small framed black-and-white photographs, behind the single cup, plate and glass on the shelf, and he stops to examine them. The photos are of someone who could be Poppy playing with three children in front of a very broad-leafed bush and a solid stone wall. The pictures are a series, taken within a few minutes of each other, and are similar apart from subtle differences. In one, the eldest child holds a ball; in the next the ball is on the ground; and in the third a dog has appeared and the children are stroking it. In all three, in the same place, standing watching them, is a straight-backed woman Cosmo does not recognize, in very fine clothes. There is something sad about these pictures, propped up on the shelf at eye level, but Cosmo is not sure what.

Suddenly the kitchen, and even the courtyard, begin to feel a little claustrophobic. The greenery needs attention; some of the plants are seriously root-bound. In the kitchen, the shelf, at eye level, with one small pan, one cup, one plate, one glass and the photos as the main focus, suddenly conveys a sense of how lonely Poppy must be, sitting here in her own small prison of isolation, looking back at just three pictures of her past.

She has often complained that her legs are too tired to go very far, and since his mama died it has become apparent that some of the shopping he used to collect was for Poppy. He has taken to doing her shopping once again but he wonders if this might be a disservice after all. Maybe forcing her to go out would give her more social interaction. It is not as if her shop generates much trade – one person every couple of days if she is lucky.

He gets up, shakes himself a little, tries to hum a happy song as he locates the jug that she uses to water her leafy cell. He'll come back and water the plants tomorrow. He looks more closely at the three photographs. The woman has to be Poppy; there is something about her that looks familiar, the way she is bent over in one, the angle of her head in another ... Now the kitchen walls are closing in again ...

Is that what he will be reduced to? Looking at pictures of his past, unable to go far, stuck in the isolation of decrepitude? Which pictures would he look at anyway? He has none, certainly none of himself. Under his mama's bed, her wedding album sits in its box, but there are none of them as a family or of him as a child. They were farmers, and cameras had no business in their lives. Their lives were about soil and toil.

He sighs. The white walls of the kitchen are better than his mama's green, though. He steps back into the corridor and out into the shop, which now feels spacious by comparison, and even the smell of mothballs is better than the aroma of age and neglect. He steps on a box of slippers, each pair wrapped in cellophane, which crinkles and splits under his weight. He kneels to put them back in the box. They are enormous, too big for anyone Cosmo has ever met, but they will have been cheap, and whoever sold them to her will likely have convinced her that she will have a monopoly, being the only stockist of slippers that size. Cosmo sniggers, but it is not a laughing matter. Someone has ripped her off because she is old and vulnerable and too trusting. He pushes the box out of his path and picks his way more carefully to the door.

Outside, the air is saturated with the smell of cooking. Every family in the village will be sitting down to a feast. Oregano is dominant, and tomatoes. His stomach rumbles. Stella made a point of saying that she wasn't open today, and she invited him to her house, as did Marina. No doubt he would have had a good time at either place but he refused, preferring to be at home for this first New Year without his mama. He knows now he was imagining that he could somehow recreate some nostalgic version of past celebrations with Mama and Poppy. Did he really want to recreate it, or did he just want time to think about the good days that have passed, mourn the loss? Not so much the loss of his mama, but of having a family he belonged to, that wanted him. The possibility of him having a family of his own now is too remote to be a consideration, and he can now add to that the fact that he may never even have companionship. Just him and the empty rooms of his house for the rest of his days.

Stella looked at him long and hard when he explained that he would stay at home, and then went and boxed him up some chicken and chips, suggesting he put the chips under his own grill to heat them up when he was ready to eat.

'That's if you are really not coming to ours to celebrate?' She pretended to be ever so slightly offended by his gentle rejection, and he loved her for that.

The bolt on Poppy's front door sinks back in place with a turn of the oversized key, and Cosmo returns to his own house, passing the table in the yard that is not laid out for a feast, the chairs leaning against it at an angle to deter the cats.

Inside, the television presents a false jollity. The voices are high-pitched and grating. Surely the people on the programme would all rather be at home with their families than in the studio with a bunch of relative strangers?

He does not reheat the chicken and chips, nor even set himself a place at the table. Instead, he peels the cardboard lid off the foil tray and sits and picks at the food with his fingers, his attention drawn to a bald-headed man playing the bouzouki whilst the cameraman zooms in and out and pans across the faces of the guests, trying to make it more interesting. Cosmo half stands for his ouzo bottle, but remembers that he finished it. Just for a second this is a catastrophe and his eyes prick with tears, but his mind, for its own reasons, brings up images of Poppy's black-and-white photographs and he realises his ouzo is rapidly filling the role that he imagines the black-and-white pictures hold for Poppy. With this thought in his mind, he finds a cup and fills it with water from the tap.

The chips would definitely benefit from being put under the grill, so he makes the effort to take a look at the stove, working out the dials and knobs, turning this and that until he can feel heat, and then he puts the chips on a wire rack and lays a place for himself at the table.

'You are not going to fall into that trap,' he tells himself. 'You give up now and you will have a very long old age.' He takes a comb from the thin shelf below the mirror by the front door and combs his sleep-tossed hair.

The smell of burning tells him the chips need attention, but only the edges of one or two have caught. He takes the tray out with a cloth, tips the contents onto his waiting plate and drops the tray again, blowing on his fingers.

'Sauce!' he says. Stella gave him a little pot of lemon sauce with the chicken. 'Ever thoughtful,' he says, and then wonders what Maria is doing today. What has she done at New Year since her own mama died? Is she sitting alone like him? And what of Thanasis? And how many others like them around the village? At least Maria can cook, and won't be eating the remains of yesterday's supper.

He turns the knob on the television to try to locate another channel, then lifts the aerial, swings his arm about, finds the right position, and hangs the aerial from the bare bulb.

It is a nineteen-sixties Finos film, starring actors who are so familiar they could be members of his family. The plot is thin but he enjoys the farce. He sits to eat, gets lost in the film and has the most enjoyable afternoon, which ends with a snooze with his feet up on the table and his head hanging back.

In the evening he feels more refreshed and, just for the exercise and a change of scenery, he decides to go for a walk. At the square, he discovers Theo has opened his doors and half the men of the village have crowded into the *kafenio*, desperate after a day stuck indoors with wives and relatives, and to a man they are complaining about the chaos at home, the things they have been asked to do, the nagging they have endured. Some complain about the cooking, others about the money they have lost at the card table, and one about the poor quality of the fireworks he spent a tidy sum on.

The atmosphere is familiar and safe, and Cosmo takes one of the few empty seats, at Petta's table. Thanasis does not appear to be there, and he wonders again how his friend spends New Year, and berates himself for never having thought to ask.

'*Hronia Pola,*' Petta greets him.

'*Hronia Pola.*'

'I am so full.' Petta rubs at his stomach. Cosmo's growls emptily in response; the remains of the chicken and chips digested as he slept.

'Be with you in a minute,' Theo says as he hurries past with a tray held high. His crown of hair bobs as he hastens his step. 'Ouzo?' he asks on his return.

'Just a coffee,' Cosmo says, and Theo is gone.

The evening passes like any other. He orders a beer after his coffee because beer is served with a plate of *meze* – olives, bread and cheese – and his stomach is rumbling. Petta tells him all about the boat he is making with his baba. As he relates the details, a little melancholy tries to settle around Cosmo's heart. Petta's words create images, offer a brief glimpse into what he never had with his own real baba, but he does not allow the feeling to settle. It is a new year after all, and he finds that somewhere in the course of the day he has made some decisions. He is not sure when they were formulated, but they are there, lurking at the back of his mind. As Petta continues to describe the finer points of the vessel he is constructing, Cosmo lists his decisions in his head:

A) I will not feel sorry for myself.

B) I will not use ouzo to stop myself feeling whatever it is I am feeling.

C) I will stop making excuses and putting off the things I am scared to do.

The new year seems to have brought him some clear thinking.

Petta is now explaining about the glass fibre that he was sanding yesterday and about how itchy it left his arms, and Cosmo decides to call it a night.

Besides, there is something he wants to do.

'It sounds interesting, Petta,' he says. 'Perhaps I will come and have a look.' He stands, stretches, finds a few coins in his pocket, leaves them on the table, and walks out into the starlit night with a wave in Theo's direction.

'And why should this year not be a year that is unlike any other you have had?' Cosmo asks himself as he walks across the square.

'Talking to yourself is the first sign of madness!'

Vasso's kiosk is not open on New Year's Day. There are no magazines out, no crates taking up the path, but she has something in her hand and is locking up the little door at the back. Perhaps she had forgotten something. Cosmo laughs at her joke, which surprises him. He does not feel defensive over being called mad, which this time last year would have left him feeling embarrassed and annoyed in equal measure. Recognising this change makes him laugh even more.

At home, he takes Poppy's oversized key, opens her shop, turns on the light and walks over to the selection of cards on the counter. He walks his fingers through them until he finds one that will do. He is not sure if he should leave the money on the counter or talk to Poppy when she returns. As the card has no price, he decides not to leave a coin but simply locks up and returns home.

At the kitchen table he opens the card and writes.

'De-ar Than-a-sis, Hap-py name day from your vill-age friends.' He speaks the words out loud as he writes.

'There,' he says, admiring his handiwork. 'Tomorrow we begin the hunt.'

Chapter 15

The sun, filtering through the thin curtains, begins to warm the room. Last night was so cold it woke him up, sending him groggy with sleep to struggle, in the early hours of the morning, with the woollen blankets in the trunk at the end of his bed. The blankets smell of mothballs and are age-worn and scratchy but at least, after a while, he warmed up and finished his dreams.

A strip of sky is visible between the top of the curtain and the edge of the window. Light blue, not the deep azure of summer. He hopes there was no frost last night. There were no warnings of frost, no talk of it in the *kafenio*, but he needs to do something about that fan he thought he had fixed. He put it on last week and to his dismay and deep concern it did not work. In a panic, he called the fan-servicing man, who insisted he was booked solid every hour until sometime next week.

'What if the frosts come before that?' Cosmo asked, but the man explained that it was not the summer now and everyone wanted their fans servicing. There was nothing for it but to wait. So, after such a cold night last night, Cosmo's priority today, after delivering the post, must be to try to fix the fan himself.

The sun has not warmed his room yet and the bare boards are cold against the soles of his feet. If he can sell the oranges before the frosts come he will invest in a rug.

The edges of the wooden stairs are smooth from decades of his feet rolling over them on the way down, sliding off onto the next step. He started doing it as a boy, enjoying the feeling on his instep, and now it is a habit that he cannot break. It is how he imagines a foot massage might feel.

The kitchen is cold too. He opens the front door, and the air outside is a little warmer, but not much. At this time of year his mama would roll the electric storage heater from the guest room and have it gently warming the corner of the kitchen. Now the thought of it burning electricity day and night seems like a ridiculous expense. Cosmo puts on his coat and fills the *briki* with water and sets it on the stove. He needs coffee before he does anything.

In the time it takes for the sugar to dissolve and the water to heat, for the coffee to be absorbed and the mixture to boil, Cosmo has surfaced enough to begin to consider what might be wrong with his orchard fan. They did have a couple of screws and a washer left over when he and Thanasis reassembled it. The fan worked when he had set it back in place, but he only tested it the once, just a burst, and did not run it for long. Maybe, he thinks hopefully, one of the power wires has come loose. He could fix that easily enough.

The bubbles on top of his small cup of coffee glisten with the dissolved sugar. He sips the hot nectar carefully and lets it slowly wake him. Halfway through his coffee, he feels his stubble. He shaved yesterday; he will not shave today. On the table in front of him is the card for Thanasis. At least that is something positive he can do, even if the fan turns out to be beyond him. Draining his cup, he puts the card in his satchel.

On the way to Saros he first hears and then sees the fan rotating in one of the orchards, but that might just be the wind catching the blades. The oranges in all the orchards look fine, and there are none on the ground. He stops at a place where one tree hangs over the road and he examines the fruit more carefully. They do not seem frost damaged. He squeezes one and is relieved to find it is still firm. He smells it: it still has that strong citrus smell. There are no spots or discolouration on it and under the tree there are no fallen leaves. All of this, of course, is no guarantee but it puts his mind at rest. It did not feel like it was minus two Celsius last night, the critical point for the oranges. But then, it is not the air temperature that he needs to worry about. The temperature between the branches of the trees can be as much as five degrees lower than just above the canopy. That is what the fans are for, to mix the air. Even turning on the watering system can circulate the warmer air from near the earth upwards, keeping the frost at bay. Tonight, of course, might be a different story, so after work his priority must be to fix the fan.

There is a lot of mail today, probably backed up over the New Year. But on the plus side it means he will visit a lot of the people he wants to sign Thanasis's card.

The air is cold on his face on the return journey to the village, and he makes a note to find his scarf. He wonders where his mama used to store the winter clothes.

'Scarf, card, oranges!' He whistles through his teeth. This time last year he would not have had a thought in his head; now his mind is constantly filled with things he must do or remember.

Sakis, as usual, has many letters, and once they are safely posted, Cosmo's satchel feels lighter. Presumably it is fan mail – they cannot all be contracts and business, can they? There is no strumming this morning; instead, a recording is being played: the grating voice of Sotiria Bellou, like marbles against the shore. It is a popular song and it stays with him as he goes next door to Dora and Yorgos's. Dora must have seen him coming because she opens the door before he has a chance to knock. Dora, despite her age, squeals like a child, exclaiming that the letter he hands her is from Yorgos's second cousin in America.

'We are thinking about visiting them. Can you imagine? Me in America!' Dora enthuses.

Yorgos smiles at her lovingly and then wishes Cosmo a good day. He is by the garden gate before he remembers the card. He feels uncomfortable asking Yorgos to sign – he would be saddened and appalled if Yorgos's writing were to match that of the anonymous love letters, but he turns back to the house anyway.

'Ah, Yorgo,' he says, 'the name day for Athanasis is soon' – he uses the formal version of his friend's name. 'Well, Thanasis the donkey breeder has been a good friend to me so I thought it would be nice to give him a card, you know, just to wish him well on his name day. I thought I would get everyone to sign.'

As he says the words he realises how ridiculous it seems. Who in the village gives cards to their friends? Sure, men to their wives occasionally, grandparents to their grandchildren, but one grown man to another? To cover the blushes he feels must be showing, he bends his head to search his bag for the card and brings it out hesitantly.

'A card?' Yorgos says, and he takes it, looking at the front, the back and then inside. 'But no one has signed.'

'I've just started.' Cosmo can feel his face burning now.

'Whatever next, eh?' Yorgos chuckles. 'I am getting old, I think, but first Marina selling Christmas decorations and now cards for our friends' name days. The village is moving with the times and leaving me behind. Do you have a pen?'

Cosmo is glad of the distraction of looking for a pen. 'Here you go.'

'It's a pretty card. And I think it is a nice idea. Why not? Good for you, Cosmo,' Dora says, looking on as Yorgos signs in a large swirling hand that Cosmo is very relieved to see is nothing like the anonymous lover's. He glances at Dora to see if she is making fun of him, but her words are sincere.

'Cheers,' he says as the card and pen are handed back.

The more houses he visits, the easier it gets to ask, and the responses are generally positive, especially from the wives. Cosmo almost forgets why he is arranging for the card to be signed, and instead begins to think how much Thanasis will appreciate the gesture. By the end of his round he has handwriting samples from all but three of the men on his list, and they seem like very unlikely candidates. One is old Aris, who is older even than Mitsos. He has been with Katerina since he was eleven; married at sixteen, they have ten children. When would he even have the time to fantasise about Maria? Another is Mitsos himself, and he is clearly devoted to Stella. The third man is Takis, who has no farm and survives by doing odd jobs in Saros. To Cosmo's mind he is a bit of a thug and he hopes for Maria's sake it is not him.

'But if it is none of these?' he says, hanging his satchel on the hook by the front door and retrieving the card. 'Then it must be one who hasn't signed.'

He takes off his coat, puts the card on the table and rubs his hands together for warmth. He is tempted to bring the heater from the other room, just to warm up the kitchen for an hour or so, or he could go straight to Stella's or Theo's.

'Oh, and Theo, so that's four. I forgot about Theo. But Theo has Anastasia.' He frowns. 'But that could be his motive – Tassia will not marry him,' he mutters to himself. 'No! He is too in love with her. It cannot be him, can it?'

But a part of him wishes it is someone like Theo. Maria deserves to be wooed by a good man. He would not wish that on Tassia, though. He plucks the card off the table and puts it on the shelf in front of the letters he has still not delivered to Maria – and perhaps never will, he admits to himself.

He cannot think about it any more. There was something pressing he needed to do. Now what was it?

Chapter 17

It is beginning to grow dark and he has not had a *mesimeri*. He yawns but he must continue. If he does not get the fan fixed there is a chance he will lose his crop. Grigoris came wandering through the trees from the next orchard earlier and called up to him that a frost was forecast for tonight.

'Panayia!' Cosmo swears as a washer slips from his grip and tinkles down the inside of the fan's upright support. That is gone for good; it is ten metres to the tube's bottom, and there is no opening. Holding tightly on to the ladder, he climbs up one more rung to look down the tube.

'Gamoto!' There is no ledge that it could have caught on; it is just straight down to the bottom. Well, it will have to be fixed without the washer.

An hour later it is almost dark and Cosmo admits defeat. Climbing down, he berates himself.

'Save a couple of euros, you said to yourself, and now you are going to lose the whole crop. Prove that you aren't lazy, you said, and now the whole village will see how useless you are. You are such a useless idiot, your mama was right.' His feet land on solid ground.

'Talking to yourself won't fix it.' It is Grigoris again, hidden in the shadows.

Cosmo does not even bother to feel embarrassed; he just feels a fool. Overconfidence – that's what his mama used to say he suffered from when he tried to do things, and that is what has let him down now.

'You are putting your fans on tonight?' he asks.

'Of course, but they won't reach all the way across your orchard.' Grigoris looks through the trees that stretch beyond what is visible.

'What am I to do?' Cosmo is speaking as much to himself as Grigoris.

'Well, in the old days they would light fires underneath the trees, keep them burning all night. Or you can just apply to the government for compensation for frost damage. You'll only come out a little less well off, and at least you are guaranteed to get paid, eventually.'

He chuckles at this, and begins to walk away. Cosmo watches him disappear in the twilight.

'Compensation!' he hisses. 'A handout!' And with energy he didn't know he had, he runs to the back fence where last year's prunings are neatly stacked, and he pulls them and drags them and gathers them in armfuls, and when his pile is exhausted he crosses over to Grigoris's orchard and takes all his prunings as well. It takes him some time, and night is upon him before the job is finished. But he cannot light the fires to see by – he must save the wood for when the temperature gets really low. He must get more wood. He has wood at home, but how to bring it here? He will think of something.

He jumps on his motorbike and heads back home. Once there, he prises open the door of the woodshed. There is a tarpaulin over the logs, and he lays this on the ground and, turning on the light in the kitchen and using this to work by, he makes a pile of wood in the tarpaulin's centre, pulls up the corners, ties it with rope, attaches this to the seat of his bike and then drives very slowly back to the orchard. He has just about got there when logs start to spill out onto the road. The tarmac has worn a hole through the tarpaulin, rendering it useless, but it has done the job well enough for him to run backward and forward for a while adding logs to each of the waiting piles under the trees.

He has also brought his mama's cooking thermometer and a blanket. He will wait until the temperature is nearly at freezing before he lights any fires. He does not have enough wood to waste any. The coldest time will most likely be an hour or two before dawn, and hopefully the temperature will not be below zero for long, or his wood will not last. He will wait and watch, and if the wood runs out he will have to rely on the watering system. This is less effective, apparently, but what else can he do? He has with him a jerrycan of petrol to get the fires going.

After a couple of hours in the dark, staying awake begins to be a problem. He tries walking about, singing and whistling the song that Sakis was playing earlier. He checks all the piles of wood. He checks the lighter he took from his kitchen. Everything is ready. He sits again and waits, and it's not long before he has nodded off.

He wakes, panicking that he has overslept. He can hear voices through the trees. The voices are not speaking Greek, so it cannot be Grigoris or any of the other farmers. He cannot identify the language. Who would be in the trees at this time of night? Whoever it is, they cannot be here for a good reason. He will call out, see what they want. But something stops him. There are several people, and they are speaking furtively, as if to avoid detection.

Cosmo tries to get closer without being seen, and he can see they have a stack of orange crates. He is almost by his rear fence now and he can see three trucks pulled up on the dirt track, two white ones and a blue one. The lights are on and the number plates are clear to see. If only he had a pen and a piece of paper – but his satchel is at the house. One of the men comes towards him and Cosmo bends down, crouching near the ground. With his hand to the floor for balance, his fingers find a twig and then, in a moment of inspiration, he writes with this stick in the dusty ground the registration number of each truck, and then shuffles back carefully so as not to smudge his handiwork.

He watches from a safe distance as the men begin to fill the crates with oranges, a few from each tree, working quietly and methodically across the orchard. The crates are carried back to the trucks and loaded on, and Cosmo feels his anger rising. Both he and Grigoris will lose some of their valuable crop if he does not do something. The village is too far to go for help, and no one will be awake now. A dog barks in the distance, and he stops to listen, noting that the men in the trees have paused in their work too.

Sounding harsh and alien in the natural environment, a strange whipping sound suddenly begins. The momentum of this noise grows, and it is echoed somewhere deeper in the orchard, until finally, as if this corner of the world is being invaded by helicopters, the noise is all-encompassing, coming from every direction. The blades of Grigoris's fans are turning at full speed, as are Yorgos's on the other side of Cosmo's orchard. The gang of men seem to relax, speaking with greater ease, and Cosmo wonders if they have chosen to come tonight, knowing that there will be a frost and that the noise of the fans will mask any sounds they make.

The fans! That must mean the temperature is below zero, and it means his crop is now at risk from the frost, as well as from the thieves. But he has an idea. He creeps around, nearer the front of the orchard, grabbing a log from one of the piles that he stacked under his trees earlier, just in case. Under the cover of the trees it is quieter and he can hear his own footsteps. Then, suddenly, he starts to bark, as aggressively and as loudly as he can. The sound travels under the tree canopies. He stops and moves to his left and barks again, a lighter bark, but more manic. The foreign voices have gone silent now. Then they speak more quietly, and Cosmo wonders if he can detect an edge of fear. He goes back to his first position and barks again, advancing towards the men. He can see them in the headlights of their own trucks, backing away slightly, looking nervous. He returns to his second position and barks manically. Now he can see the men picking up the crates they just put down. It gives him courage, so he barks more loudly still and, just because he is getting carried away, and because he's scared, he ends with a howl, looking up through the trees to the black sky, and then moves closer still to see the effect. He feels pleased with the dramatic touch, which surely sounded more like a wolf than a dog! Two of the men seem to be arguing, one pointing into the trees and the other pulling at his friend's sleeve, guiding him towards a hole in the fence.

With another tentative step forward, Cosmo's toes come up against something hard. One of the men is looking into the undergrowth in his direction, and Cosmo bends down to feel the hard thing on the ground. It is a log, and he picks it up and throws it as far as he can through the undergrowth. The man who was coming towards him changes direction, towards the noise. There are more than enough of them to overpower a couple of dogs, and Cosmo needs to do something more. On light feet, he backs further into his orchard. After the hours spent strimming around each trunk and over every root, he knows exactly where he is in the dark, and he finds his way easily back to the jerrycan and his bike. He can still see movements through the trees behind him: the men are coming. The temptation to jump on his bike and drive away is enormous. There is a tremor deep in his belly and a taste of metal in his mouth. But there is anger there too, and it fights with his fear, and the anger wins. How dare these men come in the night to take what he has spent months cultivating and nurturing?

The jerrycan makes more noise than he would like as he unscrews the top. Grit in the cap probably, but the fans are louder, and the men do not know the orchard as well as he does.

He pours a little of the petrol on the nearest pile of logs, holds his breath as he sparks his lighter – they might see the spark, they might see his face, and, worse, they might see that he is alone. But with a *whomp* the fire takes, and he quickly moves across to the other side of the orchard and repeats the process with a second pile.

The men seem to have stopped moving now. Cosmo creeps on silent feet around to the side of the men, who are talking hurriedly to each other. One is crossing himself, half turned and clearly eager to go. Cosmo looks back through his trees at the fires he has lit, which glow eerily. If he were a stranger and saw them he would not know what to think himself. The men seem undecided for a minute or two, but it's not long before one of them, evidently the leader, waves a hand and, with slumped shoulders, heads for the hole in the fence, taking a crate with him. As the others clamber through the tear in the fence, all Cosmo can think about is how each man is taking little care and the rip is getting wider and wider with each shove and jostle.

He sighs, but quietly, and watches as the men climb into their trucks and roll silently away down the slight incline, lights off. As they leave, Cosmo feels a tremor in his hands. Soon the engines start and the vehicles drive away, and he can feel himself shaking all over. He stands, runs to the back of his orchard and looks down the road in the direction that the trucks went. The road is empty, there is not a man in sight, but he can see that Yorgos's fence on the other side has been cut and Grigoris's the other way has a new opening. It looks like the army of men with their three trucks and their crates of oranges intended to make a night of it.

Now he would really like to go home to his bed. He feels drained and, if he is honest, still just a bit scared. He turns and sees the eerie glow emanating from under the trees and makes his way to the fires. They are well lit, but he must light the rest – his mama's thermometer tells him the temperature is hovering just below zero. The remaining hours until dawn are spent, thermometer in hand, going from one bonfire to the other, adding whatever wood is available, raking the embers together and trying to keep them going until the first weak change of colour in the east heralds the new day. The sun slowly (oh-so slowly) makes its way into the heavens and lifts the temperatures and Cosmo realises his work is done. The fires have all but burnt out now but the thermometer tells him the crop is safe, and so he heaves his body onto his bike and putters slowly home, where he falls onto his bed fully clothed, only to wake a couple of hours later in a panic, late for the post.

Chapter 18

With only three letters for Stella left in his bag, Cosmo considers his day done. He will take a coffee at Theo's and then go to the *ouzeri* for a well-deserved lunch.

His feet drag up the three steps to the *kafenio*, and he makes no effort to disguise his exhaustion. The place is humming, everyone talking at once, animated.

'I heard they put it up,' Grigoris says.

'I heard that too,' Nicolaos replies, 'at the feed merchant's last night.'

'Can you imagine, though, your crop gone in one night! A year's income stolen from under your nose! How would you survive? What would you eat?' says Yorgos, whose orchard is adjacent to Cosmo's.

'Hey, Cosmo, you look beat, my friend.' Petta and his baba, Miltos, are sitting with the farmers. The tables have all been pushed over to one side of the large room, arranged as if for a meeting.

'Hell of a night,' is all Cosmo can say.

'Ouzo?' Theo asks.

'Coffee.' Cosmo sits with heavy limbs, his head hanging, but looks up to find the men at the tables suddenly silent, looking back at him.

'What?' he asks, eyes flicking from one face to another.

'What, what?' Yorgos answers. 'You are the one with something to say! You are the one telling us you had a hell of a night and looking like death.'

'Ah, maybe he went to Saros, found himself a girl at last, had his first night as a real man?' Grigoris guffaws.

'I should be so lucky,' Cosmo retorts. 'I got to spend the night protecting your oranges Grigori, and yours, Yorgo. And all of yours!' He looks up at the faces. He has all the farmers' attention.

'What are you saying?' Petta speaks kindly.

'Last night. Well, I thought my oranges would freeze, so I stayed up to light fires. You know, the old way.' Cosmo wonders what they will make of this admission. He was lighting fires because he had not managed to get his fan working, despite having serviced it in the summer. Are they judging him as a fool?

A few of the older men grunt, though, remembering their own ordeals with nights of frost, before the fans became an option.

'What does that have to do with my oranges?' Grigoris is quick to ask, and a look of worry flashes across his face. 'Not a fire?'

'In this damp?' Yorgos says. The whole *kafenio* is silent, waiting.

'Come on man, tell us?' another voice says impatiently, and so he does, relating all he can remember and exaggerating only slightly the danger he was in. He certainly felt he was in serious danger, so he has to reflect that, does he not?

When he finishes there is a moment of silence as everyone takes in the news.

'They'll be back!' Grigoris says, his head hanging. 'They are here to rob us blind.'

This is met by sounds of agreement and thoughtful silence.

'We could lie in wait?' Cosmo suggests.

'And which night will they come? And how many nights must we wait?' is the answer from one of the old boys.

'We could add to the reward, if we all chip in. If the reward is enough one of them will tell on the others. They have no morals, these men!' Grigoris suggests. Some of the other farmers nod in agreement.

'Reward for what?' Cosmo asks.

'Didn't you hear? We have talked of nothing else for days! There is a reward for any information that will lead to their capture,' Petta says as Theo delivers Cosmo his coffee.

'On the house, you hero,' Theo chuckles.

'Yes, a hero! You are indeed!' Yorgos says.

Cosmo looks at the faces of the farmers to see if they are teasing, but he has never seen them look more serious. He is a hero in their eyes? Really? A hero? Well, he can fuel that fire!

'Maybe even more than you think!' he says. 'I wrote down the number plates of all three of their trucks!'

Just a fraction of a second passes as this news is taken in, and then every man calls, 'Bravo! Bravo! Bravo!' The room erupts with the noise. Those with drinks stand.

'Yeia mas!' 'Yeia mas!' A new round of cheers begins.

Theo slaps a piece of paper under Cosmo's nose. 'The reward,' he says, and he nods at the paper, encouraging Cosmo to pick it up. Cosmo looks down at the paper and reads out loud, 'To anyone who can provide information leading to the arrest of around thirty men suspected of stealing oranges in the villages surrounding Saros.'

The paper goes on to describe the men, mentioning that they operate out of three trucks, stealing oranges at night.

Cosmo looks around at the farmers' faces. 'That's them!' he says, and then he reads the smaller print that details the reward and explains how to apply for it, and he whistles through his teeth. That would buy a new fan. And a new fence! Maybe even a new bike.

'You will need to go into Saros and tell the police what you know,' one of the farmers says through the general noise and hubbub that the group is making. Cosmo finishes his coffee.

'Well, to Saros I will go then,' he says, bolstered by the attention. But as he stands, his body complains and he wonders why he does not just ask Theo if he can keep the piece of paper, and have another coffee or even go home and sleep. But all eyes are on him, and he suddenly feels responsible for everyone's harvest: the village's income is on his shoulders. Then again, his legs tremble with fatigue, which reminds him of his sleepless night and the fact that he still needs to get the fan fixed, unless he is prepared to stay up again and light more fires. And he doesn't really believe he will get the reward. Those things don't happen, do they?

'Off you go, then,' someone says, and there is a general hum of support.

'Er, do we know if there will be frost tonight?' he asks.

'No, no frost tonight,' is the general consensus, and his excuses die on his lips. Someone pats him on his shoulder, a thank you before he has done anything, and this is enough of a nudge to make his mind up. In any case, if his actions can stop his oranges from being taken, surely that is enough motivation in itself.

'But first, a man must eat,' he says as his belly rumbles.

The men all wish him well, God speed. One or two follow him to the *kafenio* door, saying they hope he gets the reward.

'See you, hero,' Theo calls after him good-naturedly.

Cosmo does not turn around, but he raises a hand and gives a little wave as he heads for Stella's to fill his stomach.

Out of the corner of his eye, he catches sight of Maria, up the lane towards the church, cats winding round her ankles and a dustpan and brush in her hand, by the bins where she deposits her rubbish. She is staring in the direction of the *kafenio*, presumably having heard the noise coming from within. Cosmo stands a little taller, striding out into the sunshine with the 'bravos' of his contemporaries still ringing in his ears. He smiles, but he does not catch Maria's eye.

'I am nearly ready to come to talk to you,' he says very quietly to himself.

As he crosses in front of the kiosk, the delicious smells of Stella's cooking are brought to him on a breeze. He needs to eat, of course, but he also wonders how much of what he experiences as hunger is in fact exhaustion from the night before.

'*Yeia sou*, Cosmo.'

'*Yeia sou*, Vasso,' he calls back as he passes the kiosk. When did he last eat? He cannot remember. He does know that even since buying his new clothes he has had to tighten his belt up yet another notch, so presumably he is not eating often enough.

Stella is behind the grill turning sausages, her slightly frizzy hair up in a messy knot at the back of her head. She has a freckle on her neck he has not noticed before, just below her right ear.

'You're early,' she says, and her voice tells him that she knows who he is and that she is smiling, even though she does not turn around.

'Is there food yet?' he asks.

'Will sausages, chips, *tzaziki* and sliced tomatoes do you?' she says, and now she turns to smile at him, but her face immediately falls.

'Oh my, you look tired. What have you been up to?' Cosmo is touched by the concern in her voice.

He has had enough excitement in the last twelve hours to last him a lifetime, and doesn't want to talk about it any more. He needs to calm his nerves and take stock, and so he just smiles.

'I'm fine, the food smells great. Thanks, Stella,' he says, and he walks through to the little dining area with its four tables, whose faded plastic cloths are as familiar as the grain of the wood of his kitchen table at home, and its wooden chairs, and a grease-smeared, glass-framed picture of a donkey wearing a hat on the wall to greet him. The small room is painted the same glossy pale green as his kitchen but he does not mind the colour here. The door out onto the street is closed and the air-conditioning unit on the back wall hums. At this time of year it blows a constant wave of warm air across the farmers. Cosmo is surprised but also delighted to see Thanasis sitting with Mitsos at one of the tables this early in the day.

'Yeia!' They greet him as one and Thanasis pulls out a chair for him to sit down.

'Well, I need to sell my oranges,' Cosmo says.

'Don't we all?' Mitsos answers.

'Yes, but the difference is that you have all done it before, and in my wisdom I have always let my mama sell ours. Who do I go to? Who is the man?'

It was not so long ago that he thought this question would scare him, first because asking it risked sounding ignorant, and second because dealing with the buyers face to face is a cause for worry. Or at least, it is the one thing that he knows concerned his mama. She would get that look in her eye, the fear that would quicken her breath and so easily come out as bad temper. In the days and weeks before she knew she must talk to a buyer, she would become tense and then remain tense until the oranges were harvested and taken away. The tension would only really pass when she was finally paid, which sometimes took up to two months. There was always a chance of not being paid at all, as everyone in the village knew – of the horror of living with nothing until next year's harvest. It is a familiar topic of conversation in the *kafenio*, and more than a few of the farmers are tied up in lengthy court cases with buyers who have not paid. The process can take years, and even if the buyers are found guilty there is still no guarantee of getting paid. It is a no-win situation; they are at the buyer's mercy.

But, as he asks, Cosmo does not feel all the tension he expected. He will find a buyer, hopefully one who can be trusted, with whom he can negotiate a fair price. The buyer will arrange workers to pick the oranges and then, paid or unpaid, no matter.

This strikes him as a strange thought. Last night he was facing danger and barking into the night to save his crops, and today he is shrugging the income aside as immaterial. His brow creases as he tries to fathom his thought process, see where his feelings have come from, and it slowly dawns on him that all the stress of the oranges, the desperate need to keep them safe last night, to keep them on the trees as each month passes, is his mama's. She taught him to think like this about the harvest, but it doesn't take much thought for him to realise that the income will not make much difference to him. His mama never really shared the money from the oranges with him anyway. She paid all the bills, of course, but he is managing those on his postal income easily enough. She sometimes paid for the food they ate, but paying for food is just a fact of life. Of course, she covered the expenses of the orchards: the strimmers, the pruners, the water, the electricity for the fan. The fact is that now the farm is paid for by his income, whereas before it was paid for by hers. Well, if he does not get paid for the oranges then he doesn't need to maintain the trees. He will put the whole farm up for sale and that will be that. He never wanted to be a farmer anyway. So, whichever way he looks at this, he remains calm.

He marvels at himself. When did he become so – well, so … He tries to think of a word to fit but comes up with nothing.

'Here you go, Cosmo. You want lemon or tomato sauce?' Stella puts a plate before him, and a basket of bread with a knife and fork wrapped in a napkin and a choice of both sauces. 'So, you are ready to sell, are you?' She takes a seat.

'Yes. Who do you trust to pay you?' He says this with a laugh, and he is not sure if it is a nervous laugh or a slightly embarrassed one. He is aware it might sound like he is calling someone dishonest whom he doesn't even know!

'Well, avoid Vladimir,' says Thanasis. 'He does not pay, I've heard.'

'Sergei is meant to be a man of his word. I used him the year before last,' Mitsos says.

'And last year?' Cosmo forks up some chips. The food is reviving him.

'Ah, well, last year …' Mitsos begins.

'Yes, but you promised not, this year,' Stella replies, her words clipped.

'Ah, did you wait, to get a better price because everyone else would have sold and the buyer would have no option?' Cosmo asks.

He has heard the farmers talk about this. This game divides the village; some take this risk, gambling on the possibility of higher prices, and others are adamant that it is tempting fate and sell as soon as they can, replenishing their depleted funds. The longer one waits, the higher the prices go as the available crop of oranges gets smaller. But wait too long and the harder frosts will come … Often the wives' nerves make the choice for the farmers, or so they say. There are one or two hard-core players who wait and wait and still have their oranges on the trees in February! They must dust them with a lot of copper sulphate to keep them hanging that long, Cosmo decides.

'You would be a fool to play that game,' Stella says, and she curls her upper lip, which Cosmo knows is a serious gesture, and an unconscious one. Still, it makes him laugh.

He covers his chuckling by adding, 'No waiting for me. I just want them sold.'

'Well, if you want them sold right now I have a good man's number. Sold my little harvest to him last week,' Thanasis says. 'We'll wander by my house after we have eaten and I will write it down for you.'

Cosmo thinks of the journey he must make to Saros – but then he recalls with a start that the licence plate numbers are still inscribed in the dust! He'll have to get those first, so he might as well go past Thanasis's place too. His heartbeat increases: what if one of the men walked over that patch of ground, or a dog, or there was condensation and they are no longer legible?

Well, finishing his lunch now will not make the difference. He takes another forkful of chips, adding a sprinkling of salt. The rest of his meal is accompanied by jolly banter and his concerns are lost in the moment. Stella is up and down, going backward and forward to the grill, keeping her eye on the chicken, making up the odd parcel of food for children who come in for their families. When Cosmo's plate is clean, it is Thanasis who stands first.

Cosmo goes to the till on his way out, to pay. 'That was good, thank you, Stella.'

Mitsos wanders with them into the grill room, Cosmo's empty plate in his hand. Once the bill is paid, Cosmo leaves, but behind him he hears Stella say, 'Such a change in that man,' and Mitsos replies with something too quiet for

Cosmo to hear that makes Stella giggle.

Chapter 19

Thanasis rides pillion and side-saddle on Cosmo's bike, and as they pull up outside his low, crumbling cottage minutes later, he slips off almost before they have stopped.

'All the beasts well?' Cosmo asks, listening to the start of a donkey's wobbling welcome. The in-breath is a sound that is so alien it is hard to believe it comes from a domesticated animal, a squeak like the sound of metal against metal that needs oiling; the out-breath is like a primitive horn, and no sooner has it started than it's curtailed again by the metallic in-breath, and then the horn – an in-breath – the horn … Ever more rapid until it becomes nothing but a series of grunts and then trails off into silence.

Thanasis has already gone around to the front of his house, which faces the orange trees. By the time Cosmo has put his bike on its stand and followed him round, Thanasis is pumping away and water is running along the maze of pipes to the trough in the yard. One or two of the animals drink thirstily; another hangs its head over the fence, where Thanasis joins it to fondle its ears. He talks quietly to the animal.

'I was told that talking to yourself is the first sign of madness.' Cosmo sits on an upturned orange crate. Over the years, Cosmo has seated himself in this compacted mud yard, half shaded by the overhanging branches, on a wooden crate, a stack of tyres, an olive oil drum, a bale of straw. Today there is a green plastic crate that has cracked down one side, and Cosmo sits with care. If the crack opens as he rests his weight, when he stands the release of pressure will make the crack close and nip his skin.

'I am not talking to myself. I am talking to Artemis here,' Thanasis replies, scratching behind the animal's long fluffy ears. After a few seconds, he looks at Cosmo blankly.

'Now, what was it that I was meant to be doing?'

Cosmo grins and opens his mouth to speak.

'Oh yes, the buyer's number.' Thanasis tickles Artemis's nose and heads for his front door.

'I swear if your cottage was any bigger you would have these beasts in the house with you,' Cosmo calls after him. Artemis looks over too, as if waiting for Thanasis to re-emerge.

Cosmo has only been in the house a few times. He recalls that the two rooms are very small; the rafters were exposed and the flagged floor was very dusty. There is an old fireplace in the first room, and a cracked marble sink set into the wall under the window. He imagines that the kitchen table will still be covered with pots and pans, all used, and in amongst the mess on the table, no doubt there will be a single-burner gas stove, the rubber tube trailing over the table's edge to a gas bottle on the floor. By the table there was also a fridge, if he remembers rightly – yes, he looked idly inside only to find it was being used to store feed for the donkeys, and was not cold.

'Keeps the mice out,' Thanasis informed him at the time.

There was a high-backed wooden chair by the fireplace, and a dark wooden chest of drawers against the far wall that looked very old. Its surface gave the impression that at one time it was polished, but dust had gathered and the piece now looked sadly out of place. Thanasis told Cosmo it was his mama's and the subject of his family was both opened and closed with that one comment. Cosmo did not go into the second room, but he could see the end of an old brass bed and huge bundles of sheets or clothes or something, both on the bed and piled on the floor.

Thanasis finally reappears, holding up a slip of paper.

'Do you have a pen and paper?' he says. 'I would like to keep a copy.'

'Er, no.' Cosmo does not have his satchel with him. This is twice he has needed his pen and notebook, and he wonders if he should start putting them in his breast pocket before he leaves the house in the morning. He scowls at the thought. The only man he knows who does this is Babis the lawyer, who has still not completed his probate.

Thanasis has gone back inside to find a pen and paper of his own, and he returns with an exercise book and an old but surprisingly fancy-looking pen – black with a band of gold around the top.

'It was my baba's,' Thanasis explains, sitting heavily on an orange crate and opening the book on one knee. It is an old book, of the sort they used at school, with yellowed pages.

Thanasis concentrates on writing first the man's name and then the number. 'If you are anything like me,' he says, 'you will lose this paper, find it again, and then wonder what it is, so I will put my name on it too, and then you will know what it is about.'

Cosmo stares through the fence at the donkeys. He frowns; something about the scene does not look right.

'I thought you had five donkeys now, since you adopted that grey one last week?' he says, tucking the piece of paper that Thanasis hands him, carefully folded, into his top pocket. 'Was she really just left by the gate?'

'Yes, can you believe it?' Thanasis is suddenly animated, and springs to his feet, eager to show off his beasts. But his steps falter.

He looks around the enclosure, yanks the gate open and runs into the pen.

'Coco?' His voice is frantic. Cosmo jumps up from his seat, expecting to see a donkey ill – lying on the ground, maybe. Instead, he sees Thanasis running into the barn and out again, around the fig tree and back and finally up to his back fence. Cosmo can see from this distance that it has been cut, just like the fence in his orchard and those next door.

Thanasis has gone, through the gaping hole and down the track. Cosmo looks left and right, wondering what he can do, and steps towards the enclosure, but then Thanasis is back.

'Gamoto! Malakes!' he swears harshly. 'They have Coco.'

His face suddenly looks drawn and old, and Cosmo thinks his friend's eyes are misting over. His energy is gone and the man has the air of someone defeated.

Cosmo is going to ask who 'they' are, but he suspects that it is the same 'they' who cut his fence into his orange grove.

'They tried this a few months ago,' Thanasis says. 'I found the fence half cut, as if they were coming back to finish the job.' His eyes are definitely misted over, a shiny streak running down his cheek.

'Do you think we disturbed them?' Cosmo says. It seems odd that just one donkey was taken. But Thanasis does not answer.

Artemis nudges the old man in the back with her soft nose and Thanasis's hand automatically fondles her ear before he slumps to a sitting position on a log.

First the oranges and now donkeys. Cosmo opens his mouth to blurt out all he knows, but then closes it again as he looks at his friend who, for all the world, does not look like he could take in one more piece of information. His head rests on Artemis's nose and his eyes are blank, as if he sees nothing. It will not help Thanasis unless the thieves are caught and then – well, maybe they can get the donkey back. Cosmo's determination gathers inside him like a steel knot. He must get going to Saros to tell the police of the registration numbers. But looking at his friend in his sadness, he finds he cannot leave. Maybe telling him what he knows will help?

'Ah my friend, life is cruel,' Cosmo begins. 'I imagine they are the same thieves that threatened the oranges.'

'Probably,' Thanasis mutters, but the word is an automatic response. He sits slumped, no longer responding to Artemis's nudging.

'Can I get you anything? You want some water?' Cosmo feels at a loss. Thanasis does not answer.

Thanasis sits in silence, Cosmo crouched by him. The hum of bees and the rasping of crickets fill the orange grove. Occasionally, one of the donkeys moves, a step or two, but otherwise there is silence. They continue like this for a time until Thanasis stands without warning.

'Okay, she is gone, what can I do?'

But Cosmo knows it is he who must do something.

'Maybe I can do something. I must run,' he says. If he gets to the police sooner rather than later, maybe they will catch the men, even find the donkey. It's a possibility ... Although the donkey may have been sold on already, or even stolen to order. That too is possible.

'They probably put her in a truck and drove away. There were no hoof marks,' Thanasis rambles.

Cosmo has visions of his mama in her coffin, the lid being slid on outside the church, and then the bearers manoeuvring the box into the back of the hearse. The steady stream of villagers walking behind the car to the graveyard, dark suits, hands crossed in front of them, heads bowed.

'I will do all I can to get Coco back for you.' Cosmo feels in his pockets. He needs a pen and paper to write down the registration numbers of the trucks.

'Please don't let the wind or the dew have taken them,' he mutters, taking out the piece of paper folded in his top pocket. He opens it out to remind himself what it is and tries to concentrate. His eyes narrow to see more clearly – then they widen, and he steps back so fast he kicks over an orange crate.

'Been stung?' Thanasis asks, his eyes still staring, unseeing. But Cosmo can only stare at the paper, with the name of the orange buyer, and his phone number. Thanasis's spidery writing is all too familiar, as is the paper, which is lined, with a stain in the top left-hand corner.

'You all right?' Thanasis says, this time looking up and shading his eyes with his hand.

But Cosmo is speechless and cannot reply. He is also breathless; he has forgotten how to breathe. Eventually, he takes in air again, a huge lungful, but still he cannot say anything; he just stares first at the sheet and then at Thanasis.

'What?' Thanasis pats Artemis's nose – a gentle, kind motion.

Still Cosmo cannot speak. What would he say? His instinct, strangely, is to run. To get away.

'Gottago,' he slurs and, notepaper in hand, he turns and makes a dash around the outside of the house, starts up his bike without kicking up the stand and then tries to accomplish this as his machine speeds him off, swerving down the road.

'Nooooooo,' he hisses in the wind, but does not make another sound until he is inside his own house with the door shut. Only then, in the privacy of his own kitchen, does he allow himself the freedom to react. But how to react? He walks to the sink, back to the door, looks at the slip of paper, at Thanasis's handwriting, walks to the sink again. He runs the tap to fill a glass, puts it down without drinking, walks to the back door, returns, takes a deep noisy breath, and wipes his hand over his forehead and back over his hair. How on earth is he meant to feel? He takes down the letters and smooths them on the table, puts the paper with the orange buyer's number next to it. They are a perfect match. The spidery writing, the lined paper, the stain – it is all there.

'Thanasis!' He says his friend's name out loud as if he has never heard it before. 'Of all the people.'

He marches to the front door, turns round, marches to the back door. What is he supposed to do now?

After a few more minutes' pacing, the initial shock has worn off a little and he begins to consider his friend in a way he has never considered him before.

'Is he a good man?' he asks, one hand on either side of the sink, looking down into the plughole.

'Of course he is a good man.' He answers himself quickly, but the answer does not sit entirely well. He is a good man for a friend, but is he a good man for Maria? Now that is a different question. Isn't it?

'What has Thanasis got to offer?' he asks the *briki* on the shelf, looking up from the sink, confident that this is a safe question with an easy answer. But he thinks again. What *does* he have to offer? In a material sense he has a small orange grove and four donkeys – at the moment – and a cottage he could never imagine Maria even entering, let alone living in. Thanasis has no other assets and no money, to Cosmo's knowledge. He gave all he had to educate his two nephews.

'But Maria has her own house and a small annuity, so perhaps counting Thanasis's assets is not the right way to phrase the question. Maybe it is more a question of character?'

There, now he feels confident this will be an easy one to answer in Thanasis's favour. He hitches up his trousers on his narrowing hips.

'He is wise, or at least he knows things. Well, he should, he has been around long enough.' He begins to laugh at his joke, then slaps a hand to his mouth. How old is Thanasis anyway? Older than he is himself by a long way – older than Mitsos, even. Surely he isn't sneaking into his eighties!

'Ha, age! What is that? Nothing in the way of love. No, his character, what does he have to offer in terms of character?'

Cosmo pushes away from the sink and turns. He is now facing his mama's cuckoo clock, which has remained unwound and silent since the day she died. He must give it to Poppy. Poppy would love it.

'Stop distracting yourself! Think, man, think.' But the more he applies himself, the less he can see what Thanasis has to offer Maria.

Will Thanasis be loyal to her, he asks himself, and he answers, Who knows? Will he be attentive? Who knows? Will he put her before his donkeys? Probably not. Will he offer good conversation? Again, probably not. He likes to play *tavli* and let Cosmo do the talking. Does Maria even like *tavli*, and does it matter? Thanasis had an interesting life when he was younger. But then, what does that have to do with now? He cannot entertain Maria for the rest of her days with repeated tales of his youth.

Cosmo paces once more to the back door, trying desperately to think of what he does or does not have to offer Maria himself. Poppy's key hangs on the nail there by its red twine. He plucks it off. Now is as a good a time as any to water her plants; after all, in his current state of mind he is not much use for anything else.

The shop door opens easily and he is glad of the distraction. The mothball smell is comfortingly familiar and nothing to do with either Thanasis or Maria. The smell of tuna is fainter in the house now, and it might be the drains, or stale clothes. In the kitchen all is still. Today, with no one to stir the air, it smells ever so slightly damp. He fills the jug and opens the door to the tiny courtyard that brims with green leaves around the single, comfortable-looking chair. The leaves on some of the plants droop a little, and he waters every pot carefully. If he were to construct a container of some kind to perfectly fit the space, the plants could be replanted into the larger container so the roots would have more room. Maybe he will talk with Poppy about that when she gets back.

After several trips back and forth to the tap he sits amongst the now-revived plants and looks through to the kitchen, at the shelf with the small pan, the one plate, the one cup, the one glass. Underneath, the pictures of Poppy and the children, with the smartly dressed woman looking on, stare back at him. What is so sad about these pictures? He still cannot work it out.

He stands and makes his way back to his house, closing and locking the doors carefully.

With the watering distraction gone, the question still remains – is Thanasis a good man for Maria?

Chapter 20

'Arrogant,' he says to his reflection as he combs his hair in the small mirror by his front door. He replaces the comb on the shelf and continues to look himself in the eye. 'Who am I to decide if Thanasis is right for Maria or not? What if you decide not, and you cause her to miss her soulmate?'

He shakes his head at his reflection. His kitchen is driving him mad. It is not quite the same green as Stella's eatery after all, but a decidedly more sickly shade. He goes through to the room his mama kept only for visitors. The air in here is still, the aging furniture squeezed in, so cramped. The plastic flowers in the bowl on the small glass coffee table are thick with dust. Now, this is a good distraction. He goes back to the kitchen, takes a plastic bag from the corner behind the door and returns to wrap up the flowers, carefully, leaving the dust undisturbed. He throws the bag out of the back door. Someone has left a chair outside Poppy's. No doubt when she comes back she will put a price tag on it. This gives him an idea, and almost before it has time to settle, his mama's prized glass-topped table is next to the chair, and the best room feels just a little more spacious.

He sits in one of the plump seats, but there is no give to the springs; it is most uncomfortable and, being without arms, it offers nowhere to rest his hands.

The problem of Maria will not leave him be.

'Firstly, you are not meant to know who the letter writer is,' he reasons. 'So from that point of view you should not interfere. No one has invited you to get involved.'

He crosses his arms. 'But I do know. Fate, circumstances, call it what you like, but whatever it is has brought this knowledge my way. Doesn't that mean I have a responsibility to use my knowledge wisely? Don't I?' He uncrosses his arms.

A spring is digging into his backside so he moves to another chair. This one has more give but one would not call it comfortable.

'It's not as if it was my efforts that allowed me to find out who it was. It was chance, not the card. I could just go to Maria and give her the orange man's number with Thanasis's handwriting and tell her that Thanasis gave me it and she will say, "What do I want with that, I have no oranges?" But then she will look again and see, and it would come to her and I would not have to say a word. I could walk away and then I would have no choices or decisions to make.'

Next, he tries the two-seater sofa, which also has no arms, so he cannot lean sideways. He feels very upright, sitting to attention. It is worse than the chair. What sort of chair would he buy if he had the money? Maybe one like Babis has in his office – a big black one that swivels. Or maybe a sofa, like the one Juliet, the English woman in the village, has out on her patio in the summer – a big, squashy thing that he could fall asleep on. But he has what he has and it will have to do. The seat is too uncomfortable, and his legs are restless. He will be better on his feet.

With a last look he closes the door to the unused – and unusable – room behind him. Next time he goes in there he will bag up all his mama's fussy little ornaments. Poppy will love those.

'But just giving Maria the note is a decision! Maybe it is best not to make a decision after all, do nothing.' His guts twist at this thought. He promised himself that he would stop making excuses about the things he is scared to do. But what if he gets it wrong? What then?

Normally, he would not think of this as a question to be answered, but today he considers it.

'What would actually happen?' he asks himself. 'What would be the worst-case scenario? Maria might fall out with me and Thanasis would not be so friendly?'

He says this out loud whilst internally he asks himself, *Is that true?* Thanasis is not one to hold a grudge. He might say that he, Cosmo, was in the wrong for interfering, but it would not break their friendship. As for Maria, he would lose an hour or two a week in her company reading her letters, and even that would not be forever, just until enough time had passed to smooth everything over. So probably he would not lose anything. What would be the gain? Thanasis and Maria might have a happy-ever-after, or, better still, Thanasis might be rejected by Maria and then he and Maria could have their own happy-ever-after. A lot to gain, potentially.

So that is settled, he will take some action. But in which way?

'Enough!' he declares. 'My head is going to explode.' And he stomps from the house to the *kafenio*.

'Ah, here he is. What did the police say?' This greeting confuses him, and he looks behind him to see who is being addressed, before recalling all of a sudden that when he last left the *kafenio* it was to go to the police in Saros with the registration numbers of the thieves' vans! He puts a hand over his mouth – he hasn't even been to write down the numbers that are still –

hopefully – scratched into the dirt in the orchard. He must do that, and quickly, if it isn't already too late. His foot does not even touch the last step, and he swivels and trots back down, runs to his house and jumps onto his bike, satchel over his shoulder.

At the back of his orange orchard the dust is untouched; no breeze has stirred the ground and his twig scribbles are clear. He copies the letters and numbers and before anything can interrupt him again he is on his way to Saros.

By the time he finally comes out of the police station, his stomach is rumbling as if he has never been fed. He watched the desk sergeant eat a salami and salad sandwich and wash it down with a cola, before being ushered to an inner room where he sat with a detective someone-or-other who was eating a sugary doughnut, and drinking what smelt like a strawberry milkshake. His doughnut sprinkled sugar onto the official form he was filling out, and when the detective wiped it away with his sleeve it left a faint trace of grease across the words in a sweeping arch.

Cosmo told his tale four times in all, and the third time it was written down by a girl with false eyelashes and long fingernails that made it very difficult for her to type. But he was glad she took her time because her police shirt was undone enough to show the edges of her black bra, which caused him some trouble in concentrating on what he was saying.

Finally, the lawyer representing the farmers who had put up the reward turned up, and Cosmo took out his notebook again, and told his tale again, and the lawyer made a note of the numbers, quizzed Cosmo for a description of the men and made him sign a declaration.

'Do I get the money now?' Cosmo asked. People seem constantly to be hiring lawyers, taking each other to court, tangling each other up in red tape. But how often does one hear of a positive outcome, of debts being paid, or settlements being honoured?

'Got to catch them first,' the lawyer said, and stuffed his papers away in his briefcase. Cosmo sucked his teeth and the lawyer left and he was alone. He sat for twenty minutes before he realised that he had done all he was meant to do and could leave. No one else wanted to speak to him, no one thanked him, no one showed him out. He stood and left the room, his notepad forgotten on the table.

'See you,' he called to the desk sergeant, who was now crunching away on a bag of nuts, but the man did not even look up from his newspaper.

If he does ever get the reward money, and judging by the lawyer's demeanour this now seems like a big 'if', but if he does, might there be enough for a new chair as well as a new fan and a fence around the orchard?

His bike coughs and is reluctant to start, and only splutters into life after much coaxing.

He is ravenous as he pulls to a stop outside the eatery and he hopes he will not have to wait long for his chicken and chips.

Heaving his bike onto its stand, Cosmo calls *'Yeia sou'* to Grigoris, who is passing on his tractor, and his thoughts turn once again to Maria. With all the officialdom of the police station and his focus on producing a factual statement, he is thinking logically, and he realises that he is in no position to second-guess what a fifty-year-old woman might think of Thanasis. How does she see him? He doesn't have a clue. It would be useful to talk to a woman about this. He needs to talk to someone nearer Maria's age. Not Poppy, she is too old, but someone who is discreet. Someone who is …

'*Yeia sou*, Stella.' His eyes light up at the sight of her, a perfect choice.

'It seems your belly is never full these days,' she jokes. It is true, but unless he learns to cook he will continue to eat here every day. Of course, he is here for the company as well as good food.

He goes through to the dining area but there is no one there. It is the in-between hours.

The lunch farmers have gone for a sleep and the evening diners have not yet arrived.

'Mitsos not here?' He comes back into the grill room, where Stella is shaking a bottle of a thick, pale-yellow liquid, a new batch of her lemon sauce.

'Up at the house – do you need him?'

'Actually, no.' He scratches his head. Now how does he start?

'Troubles?' she asks, putting the bottle down.

'No. Well, yes. Well – sort of. Advice would be good, you know, because you are a woman and – well, it's complex and I am not sure what to do.'

'Oh.' Stella becomes animated. 'You want to sit?'

Just at that moment his stomach gurgles so loudly that neither of them can ignore it. Stella takes a plate and starts piling it with chips.

'Sausages or chicken or both?' she asks.

'Everything! Tomatoes, salad, pile it all on.' He takes a beer from the fridge, cracks it open with the opener that hangs on a string from the fridge door, throws the cap in the bin and goes back through to the little dining room. Stella is right behind him, carrying a basket of bread, cutlery and a plate of food.

'You are an angel,' he says, and before he can stop himself he has shovelled in several mouthfuls of food and can hardly close his mouth to chew. The olive oil on the tomatoes is so fresh and thick he could eat a plate of it on its own and be happy. It must be the first oil of the season. Stella sits at the table with him and watches him eat, smiling.

'God, I am so hungry,' Cosmo says as he swallows his mouthful, then he washes it down with the beer. Soon the urgency subsides and he sits back a little. Stella is still waiting for him to talk.

He dabs at the corners of his mouth with a paper napkin – the lemon sauce has a tendency to go everywhere. He checks his shirt front, but he is fine, he has not spilt any.

'Here's the thing.' He pauses. How should he express himself? 'I know someone who is admired by someone. But this someone does not know who this other someone is. But I have happened to find out who this other someone is. So, do I tell this someone who the other someone is, or do I let the other someone keep their secret because if they wanted the someone to know they would have told the first someone?'

Stella frowns and pulls down the corners of her mouth. 'Complex?' she says. 'Unintelligible!'

'Did you not follow? Someone is admired by some–'

'Stop!' says Stella, laughing. 'It is all the someones that I cannot follow. Who is the object of attraction? A woman or a man?'

'A woman.' Cosmo feels he should be cautious. He does not want to let on whom he is talking about.

'Okay,' says Stella. 'Let's call her Maria. That's a common enough name, it could be anyone.'

Cosmo almost chokes on his chips at this. He takes another swallow of beer and controls himself. For a moment he thought she had guessed, but he scans her face and sees that she is looking beyond him, deep in thought. The sun is low in the sky now and it is piercing the room with soft orange shards that cut across her face, light up her gold earrings, make the flecks in her eyes stand out.

'So, Maria is admired by – let's pick a name. Yianni. But he has not told her?'

'No, he has not told her. He has admired her for the best part of thirty years and she knows someone admires her but she does not know who.'

'Are they both single?' She is looking at him now, and the slight smile that plays at the corners of her mouth lets him know that she thinks he is the admirer. Which of course he is, in a way, but not in the way she thinks. He cannot add that to the mix, that would really confuse her.

'Oh yes, yes! This is all above board and proper. They are both unattached.'

'Okay, so you knew she had an admirer, and somehow, I will not ask how, but somehow you have discovered it is Yianni.' She gives him a side-on look, eyebrows raised. 'For the sake of a better name.'

'Er, Yianni, yes, right.' He uses some bread to soak up the juices of the tomatoes that have mixed with the oil at one side of his plate.

'So, should you tell her?'

'That's the question.' He exhales, relaxes a little. She is bound to know what to do.

'Depends on the man – who this Yianni is.' She sits back, looking at him directly, challenging him.

'Does it?' he responds. He has never thought of Stella as intimidating before, but right now he feels just a little scared of her. Or does he just feel annoyed that he is back to the question of whether Thanasis is a good man?

'Why does it depend on who Yianni is?' he asks.

'Well, some men are worth being admired by, worth considering, and some would just be an amusement.'

'Ah.' This doesn't seem to be getting him anywhere.

'Well, if it was you, for instance …'

So she does think it is him.

'No, it is not me. Not until the way is clear,' he says, and then he looks up sharply. He has said too much.

'Aha, so that is your involvement.' Now she smiles broadly. 'So you admire someone, who is admired by another. You feel he has the first rights on her and so you want to know if you should tell her about him or just make a move yourself?' Stella tips her head to one side.

'Oh no, I couldn't just make a move myself.' He looks around himself furtively, to reassure himself that no one is listening in to their conversation. Stella responds by moving a little closer to him, encouraging him.

'Why not?' Her voice is soft.

'Well, this person has been writing for thirty years.'

'Ah, writing.' She leans back as if everything is clear to her now. Then she leans forward, with a slight frown, concerned. 'And you have delivered these letters? And read them to the woman, I suppose?'

Cosmo looks up sharply at this.

'Oh, come on,' Stella continues. 'I know half the village cannot read or write. It's no secret to me! You must have died a little every time you had to read one of these letters.'

She puts her hand on his, just for a second, just to show she cares. She has such a tender, good heart and he has always felt an affinity for her. They were both pushed around and picked on by the other children at school – he because he was slow, and she because she was from gypsy stock. Neither of their early lives was easy. But there has always been an unspoken bond between them. Each knows what the other has suffered.

'It wasn't easy reading them.' He drops his guard; his chest feels heavy.

'Oh, poor Cosmo. And presumably you had to write her replies? That must have been awful!'

'Oh no, there were no replies. Maybe if she knew who it was, but he has never signed them, you see, in thirty years.'

'But you worked out who it was?'

'Oh no, it was chance,' he stammers. A heat comes to his cheeks.

'Is this you thinking that the other person might be a better match for her than you, by any chance, Cosmo? Because, if you don't mind me saying, that would be typical of you, and rather foolish.'

Stella gets herself a beer from the fridge. 'You want another one?' she asks.

He shakes his head. He has been called foolish before, foolish and slow, and there he was, thinking that he was changing.

'Oh, don't look so down. You have a good heart, Cosmo, but putting other people before yourself is not always the right thing to do. What of your own happiness? I say you should tell her that she has an admirer. But I think you should tell her it is you. Give yourself the chance of a happy match – why not? Do you think this other admirer deserves happiness more than you? I think not!'

With this, she gathers up his empty plate and takes it with the bread basket through to the sink in the grill room. She returns with a bottle of ouzo and two glasses.

'You want a nip?' she says.

The weight in his chest is accompanied by the weight of the food in his stomach and the weight of the world on his shoulders. Why does life have to be so complicated?

Stella talks on but he is only half listening now. He has laid off the ouzo for the last few days and the first measure makes his head spin. Stella pours another.

It would be just plain wrong to make his feelings known to Maria before she knows about Thanasis. It would be like going behind his friend's back. But he cannot tell Stella the other suitor is his best friend. What a mess. He picks up the glass, and with a quick movement his head is back, his drink is gone.

'*Yeia*, Stella!' someone calls from the grill, and two farmers come through to the dining room. They have brought their wives – to give them a break from cooking, perhaps? If he could take Maria out, Cosmo thinks, he would find somewhere in Saros, a place fit for a queen. He is not sure he can imagine Maria eating here.

The moment the farmers enter, Stella is on her feet, wiping the faded plastic tablecloth at the next table for the new arrivals.

'I must get going,' Cosmo tells Stella, and he buys a bottle of ouzo to take with him. She only has Ouzo Mini, which is not as smooth as Plomari, but it will do.

He makes a point of not going past the *kafenio*, instead taking the road behind the bakery. Thanasis might be in the *kafenio*, and he will want to play *tavli* and chat. He could not face that now. His guilt mixes with a feeling of embarrassment and a sense that his urge to take something of life for himself means he is greedy.

The whole combination causes him to spit out an accusation at himself: 'Traitor! What sort of friend are you?'

Another two shots of ouzo at the kitchen table help take the edge off these intense feelings. Another one and he has energy, and he uses it first to bag the ornaments in the best room; then, the alcohol speeding through his veins, he manhandles the two uncomfortable chairs and the sofa out of the back door and leaves them outside Poppy's with the abandoned chair and his mama's glass table. Hands on hips, he decides they look much better there.

Back inside, the sitting room is all space and emptiness. Taking the ouzo from the kitchen, he abandons his glass and sits in the middle of the empty room swigging from the bottle. His energy now drains quickly, his limbs become heavy again, and he lets them hang without a thought for his new clothes.

Then, with sudden blinding clarity, the pictures from Poppy's house spring to mind, and he sits up quickly.

'That's it! That is why the pictures are sad. It is not Poppy, it is not the children, but the woman, the woman standing at the side watching.'

He recalls the pictures as best he can. The children had her face, the same long limbs, the same hair. They were her children, and yet there she was, not playing with them, not tossing the ball and laughing. No, a young Poppy was doing that. The mother was standing and watching.

'A bystander in her own life,' he says out loud. 'That is what was so sad!'

And in the pit of his stomach, somewhere under his solar plexus, the truth twists a knot that blinds him and makes his head spin until he reels back, crashing to the floor, for he has been doing exactly the same thing. Watching Thanasis woo Maria, going about the village reading about lives that are not his, writing letters to loved ones that are not his loves, calling this his job, when in reality it is a substitute. He is participating from the sidelines in other people's lives, instead of living his own.

'Mama! Is this is your doing?'

When was his life not about her, when she was alive? When he was a boy, her thoughts and feelings were paramount in the home and his baba bowed to her every whim, or else made excuses to spend time in the sanctuary of his orchards. Mostly in the orchards. So it became his job, her son's, to keep her happy.

'Who is my little boy, my baby!' she would say, pinching his cheeks. All very well when he was six, but to still be doing it when he was thirty-six? At what point do you turn around and say no? He tried when he was fifteen or so, but she first became angry, saying he was ungrateful not to want his mama's love, and then she tried all the more to cuddle him and kiss his cheeks, half joking, but as he resisted she became quiet and stern. When his baba eventually came home he saw how sullen she was and Cosmo was in trouble.

'Being your mama is her role in life. You are trying to take this away from her?'

Cosmo's baba was not angry, but his disappointment was worse than if he had been. So, to comply and keep the peace – and after all, he had his own life waiting ahead of him (didn't he?) – he accepted the cheek pinches, the baby talk, allowed her that power, that control. In his heart, though, he blamed his baba. Why did he not save him, act as his ally and help him become a man? And if he had been more attentive as a husband, more loving to his wife, then she might not have needed to use her son as a substitute for her thwarted emotions.

Cosmo tries to take a swig of ouzo, still lying down, and it runs over both his cheeks and into his hair. 'It was all about you, Mama. It has always been all about you, to keep you pacified.'

But how her affection faded when his baba died; how quickly that supposed love turned to anger, and how suddenly his job – and it was his job – changed from consoling her to pacifying her temper, just for a quiet life, not realising that the more indispensable he made himself to her, the less likely he was to ever have a life of his own.

'She is mourning the loss of her soulmate.' Poppy pulled him to one side, on the way back to the house, after the forty-day memorial service for his baba. He and his mama had argued the night before, shouted at each other so loudly that Poppy was not the only neighbour to hear.

'She has nothing but thirty or forty years of loneliness to look forward to. She has lost her role as wife and now you take away her role of mama. Can she take no strength from her son?' Poppy looked stern but her eyes watered too, and he knew she was only trying to help.

'Ah, poor woman,' he overheard someone say later that day, as he was passing Marina's shop and, to his shame, he loitered unseen, purposefully eavesdropping. 'At least she has a son to lean on.'

'If she *can* lean on him,' another replied, and he felt offended that whoever it was saw him as undependable, so he made up his mind to be his mama's support until she got over the shock. After that, he held his tongue and minded his manners and tried to ease and smooth her life every hour he was awake, and now he is in his fifties with no life of his own.

'No more!' he shouts at the ceiling. 'Now it is my time. Me! You hear? Me!' And he rolls onto his belly and from there onto all fours, and from his knees, using the wall for support, to standing.

He will use Thanasis's method. He will write her a letter. He will tell Maria of his own love, stop thinking about other people for a while, and express his own needs. Yes! He should have done this years ago, before he knew it was Thanasis.

The wall proves to be a good support all the way to the kitchen, where he takes his pen from his satchel and is somewhat surprised to find his notebook is not there. In his mind's eye, he can see it sitting on the table at the police station, open at the page with the registration numbers.

'Gamoto!' he curses, and he drops the pen, then bends to pick it up, loses his balance, grabs at a chair to hold himself upright. Gripping hard and moving slowly, he retrieves his ballpoint and manages to sit.

Pen in hand, he looks at his paper and then remembers for a second time his notepad is gone, curses again and examines the paper Thanasis wrote the buyer's phone number on. The back is blank, that will do. He will explain. Explain how he feels, how he has felt for years, why he and Maria would be good together, the care he will lavish on her, how he has been readied to be attentive to the emotional needs of a woman. Yes, that's good! When he has finished he will post it. No, wait – he will slip it under her door, and she will see it sooner that way.

My love for you … He writes slowly, savouring this putting into words of the feelings he has kept silent for so many years.

'For too man-y years I have stay-ed si-lent …' He reads aloud as he writes, his head bowed in concentration. Finally, a letter of his own, speaking the things in his heart. He seems to have so much to say, so much to express …

He writes and writes, and his heart feels such release. He did not know he had so much to say, and he keeps writing until he runs out of paper.

Folding it carefully, the next step is to put it under her door – if he can manage to stand, of course!

Chapter 21

It sounds as if someone is pouring concrete onto a metal sheet outside. Cosmo opens his eyes but does not recognise the ceiling. His bed has grown very hard. He rolls his head, the room sways and spins, he might be sick. The room he is in is completely empty. It is his mama's best sitting room, and there is nothing in it. Has he been robbed? Small pieces of the previous evening return – memories of gouging a piece out of the back door frame with the leg of the sofa as he took her furniture and left it in the street. The village will think he has gone mad!

'Ohh!' He closes his eyes and rubs at his forehead. The softness of the light tells him it is early. Who would be pouring concrete at such an hour, and why on metal? He will tell them to stop, just for an hour or two until he feels a little better. He rolls onto his knees and crawls to the window, lifts the white, embroidered curtain and looks out. The brightness of the sun makes him squint.

He groans at the world and then peeps through one half-open eye. His mama's furniture is arranged around Poppy's front door just as it was in the house, with the glass table in the middle, the plastic flowers, still in the bag he wrapped them in, taking centre stage, and the chairs arranged as if to welcome guests. It is the oddest sight in the world and he has to stop looking because he does not want these confusing thoughts.

Left and right, up and down the street, there is no sign of a cement mixer, and as he listens hard to work out which direction the noise is coming from, he realises it is inside his head.

'Panayia mou.' He rubs at his temple. 'Never again.'

For a moment he thinks of standing, going to the kitchen and brewing up a strong coffee, but with the first small attempt it is clear his legs will not take his weight, not with the floor wallowing around as it is doing. Work is obviously going to be out of the question today, and the way he is feeling he cannot even find the inclination to care.

How long it takes him to get to the kitchen he is not sure, but with every change in direction he is sure he will be sick or that he might do permanent damage to his brain, which has taken to knocking on his skull with each movement. The idea of sitting at the kitchen table has become very appealing – he has always felt fine sitting at the table. But actually getting onto a chair proves to be a challenge. If he takes it slowly, inch by inch, eases himself around, holding the table edge …

There! He smiles, impressed with his accomplishment. He is sitting.

His pen is in the middle of the table. Why is that there? He always puts it away, one of his personal rules. How many pens he lost when he first started the job, leaving them here and there! He always puts it away. But why is it out at all?

The answer first begins to show itself as a small black dot at the back of his mind, and then, so very slowly, it grows and grows to reveal the truth to him – so slowly that by the time he is fully conscious of having written the letter to Maria he is already looking around the kitchen to remember where he put it when he finished it. It is not on the table. Surely he was not so drunk as to put it in his satchel? That would have been foolish. Someone at the post office might have found it, or, worse still but highly unlikely, he might have posted it by mistake.

The ridiculousness of this thought makes him snort, but this one slight noise makes it more than apparent that allowing himself to laugh will worsen the painful throbbing in his head that has taken over from the pouring of the concrete. Now someone is in there, relentlessly beating a giant drum, and it is almost more than he can bear. He needs a painkiller. He bought some the morning after the last time he brought a bottle of ouzo home. Where did he put them?

'Oh yes,' he whispers, and negotiates his way, slowly, to the shelf over the sink, and manages to grab the pill bottle and run himself a glass of water and sit back down again, without mishap – just a great deal of swaying and squinting.

'Never again,' he whispers, and he takes two painkillers with a large glass of water.

'Right. What was I doing?' he asks the empty glass. Oh yes, the letter. He can remember how good it felt to write it, but he is curious to read what he wrote. It must be in his satchel after all, which he can reach from his seat. He pulls it from its hook and shakes it out. Nothing! Now he frowns.

'In the bin,' he says with a wave of relief, and makes his way over to it to check. But the bin is empty except for the cap of the ouzo bottle.

'Behind the coffee packet?' He looks up at the shelf, but it is not there. He checks his pockets. His concern is increasing, but physically he is feeling slightly better, so he runs himself another glass of water and decides to be brave and try to make coffee.

He puts the little pan of water to boil on the single-burner gas stove and watches as the sugar dissolves. Once the water is clear, he adds a heaped spoon of coffee grounds and waits for the mountain of dry power to be absorbed by the water. Just as the last of the fine brown grounds sink, the realisation comes to him with the force and impact of a donkey's kick. It is not so much a realisation as a memory, isn't it? The memory of posting the letter he wrote under Maria's door.

The coffee boils over. He snaps the gas off. He cannot have posted it – that must have been a dream! He would not be so rash. Would he?

How to tell dreams from reality? It was dark, he had held on to the wall for support. That feels like reality. A cat had come, he had talked to the cat, and the cat had answered, hadn't it? That is a dream. He stumbled at the corner – reality. The church bells rang in his ears, but the church bells would not ring in the middle of the night, so it must have been a dream ... When he opened Maria's gate he caught the sleeve of his new shirt and tore it!

He inspects his right sleeve and breathes a sigh of relief. So it was a dream. He glances at his left sleeve. Horror! It is torn! No! Please, God, no, let it not be true.

Did he put it right under the door, or maybe just half under? Could he get it back? How could he get it back? But the realisation of the stupidity of his actions makes rational thinking impossible, and for a moment he curses himself and bangs his head, but very gently, against the shelf's edge.

'Be practical.' He forces himself to stop. 'Think, man. What can you do?'

He could deliver the mail and, when she opens the door, hopefully find she has not seen it, there on the floor. He can quickly put his foot on it, kick it back outside and pick it up when he leaves. It might work, if he delivers her mail first, before she is fully awake.

Suddenly he has never felt more sober and alive. His headache has yielded to this new emergency: everything is geared towards that. After a quick swill of his face at the kitchen sink and a quick drag of his comb across his hair, he grabs his satchel and leaves.

The journey to Saros to pick up the post is slightly hazardous as the road keeps moving and the sun is far too bright. The occasional tree tries to cross the road but somehow he misses them all. In the depot he is greeted by people who are speaking far too loudly, asking why he is so early, but he growls at them and stuffs the letters into his bag, checking for any for Maria. He needs at least one to Maria to make his visit to her credible. But there are none. Now what?

He will lie. Anything so Maria does not read his drunken ramblings from last night. He will take a letter and say he thought it was for her, a letter addressed to another Maria perhaps. He searches through the mail. There are none. Right, he will take any letter and say he was mistaken. She cannot read the envelope anyway, to know who it is for.

'Of course!' he says out loud, and the people working in the depot stop and look at him. He gathers up his satchel and leaves hastily. What on earth is he worrying about? She cannot read his ramblings, she cannot read at all! He shakes his head over all the stress he has caused himself.

'That will teach you to try thinking with a fuzzy head!' He laughs at himself, his dull headache reminding him how right he is. But he must go to Maria's anyway and retrieve the note, just to be safe.

The journey back is smoother than the one into Saros. The sea of tarmac has calmed, the trees are no longer suicidal and the sun has been restored to normal. The chill in the January air is refreshing. He will shave and change his torn shirt before he goes to Maria's.

Rubbing his hand on his bare chin, he breathes in the smell of the shaving foam, fresh and clean. He pulls down his shirt, sweeps a hand over his neatly combed hair and knocks.

There is silence, which he finds odd. He has always known Maria to be an early riser. He knocks again, hears a quiet step inside, and then the door opens a crack.

'*Kalimera*, Maria.' He tries not to look at the floor inside the door. If the note is there he must be subtle, put his foot on it, bend to do up his laces, something like that.

'Oh, it's you. You are early.' She opens the door wide. There is no envelope, and a wave of panic flashes through him. Now what? Maybe he is wrong. Maybe he tore his sleeve on something else and his subconscious noticed it and it came through in a dream. That happens, doesn't it?

'I'm glad you are here,' Maria says, but she does not sound happy. She leads him through to the kitchen. There is a small coffee on the table, and a plate of biscuits and – *Panayia!* – the note.

'I was just having breakfast,' she says. 'I have not touched that coffee yet. You have it and I will make another. Sit.'

Without a word, he does as he is told. He could take the note now whilst her back is turned, and, when she asks after it, feign ignorance. No, that is just stupid, she knows it is there. He wipes his forehead with his hand as she turns back with another coffee. She sits and gives him the fresh coffee, takes the one that has been standing for herself, takes a biscuit, breaks it and gives him half. He loves this gesture of hers, and now, after a single, stupid drunken night of his, when she understands the contents of the note, she will probably never do it again. He has ruined it all.

'Someone put a note under my door last night,' she says.

Every muscle in his body tightens, but concentration forces his face to remain passive.

'Really?' It comes out high-pitched; he clears his throat and takes a sip of coffee, and it leaves grit over his lips. She watches him lick it off, frowns a little.

She picks up the note and opens it out.

'Perhaps you can read it to me?'

Cosmo thinks he might be sick.

'Do you think I could have some water?' he manages.

She stands, but without haste, and seems to take a long time to get him a glass. It is still not long enough for him to think what to do. He drinks the water eagerly.

'It is here.' She hands him the note and does not blink.

'Let me see.' Cosmo tries to act as if everything is normal. He examines the letter, which is definitely in his own hand, and puts it back on the table.

'Oh, a mistake I think. It is nothing.' He takes a bite of biscuit to complete his charade.

'Maybe you are right.'

He relaxes.

'But I looked at the name at the bottom, again and again, and I think I recognise it.'

The blood rushes through his ears; stars dance before his eyes. He cannot get the hand that is holding his coffee cup to do his bidding, and the cup shakes and spills over as he returns it to the saucer.

'That's a "C", right?' She points, leaning over, her face so close. It is no longer the beautiful face of the young girl he first fell in love with. The sun has dried it, time has weathered it and age has wrinkled it, but he knows every aspect of that face, every nuance, every expression. This close he can see very fine, downy hairs on her cheek, so soft.

'And the second an "o", and then I remember the "s" from school. So far we have "Cos". Now, how will that name end, I wonder?'

And she looks at him, still close, her pupils so large and dark, all the pain and loneliness of her life expressed in the arch of her eyebrows, and the smile lines around the corners of her eyes recalling the times they have laughed together.

'Please read it, Cosmo,' she asks simply, and he feels trapped. But what else can he do? He clears his throat.

'My Dearest Beloved Maria,' he begins, and his heart screams at the truth of the words. 'My love for you I have kept hidden for too many years. Maybe I have stayed silent for too long, but my silence and keeping my love hidden has been because I suspected that you would not want my love, nor could you return it. So for you I have stayed silent. But with the passing of my mama' – he swallows hard, a lump in his throat – 'I realised we are all here for such a short time, and already so much of my life has passed with me only loving you from afar.'

He wants to look at her to gauge her reaction, but he doesn't dare, so he continues.

'I have come to realise that it would not be right for me to never speak of how I feel for you. That would be denying something that is real and intense and persistent. So I tell you now, Maria, that I love you with such a power, with such strength that I sometimes think it will engulf me. I have watched you from when you were a child, growing through all that life has thrown at you until the beauty of your womanhood has begun to fade, as all surface beauty does. But I have to really look to see that new Maria, because through my eyes your beauty is all I see, it glows from your heart, it is in the working of your mind, it is in your resilience, your dignity, your grace. Sometimes I think my ribcage will crack open to let out all I feel for you, and yet despite these feelings being so great and so powerful they only want to be expressed in tenderness – pulling out a chair for you to sit, picking you a flower, opening a gate for you to pass through, fixing that drawer in your kitchen that you need to pull so hard at just to get yourself a teaspoon.

'If I was a brave man, Maria, I would throw caution to the wind, bend down on one knee and give you all I have, if you thought it could be of any value to you.'

He stops. He cannot believe he wrote that. Part of him is delighted at his own eloquence, but most of him has drained of blood. He feels decidedly dizzy.

'You have not finished,' Maria says, and she points to the words at the bottom.

'I cannot read those,' Cosmo replies, but her steely look forces him to squeak out the last four words, very, very quietly.

'Marry me, love Cosmo.' Tears prick at his eyes. Maria has frozen; her hands do not twitch, she does not blink. Eventually, she takes the letter from his fingers and turns it over and stares at the writing on the back. Thanasis's writing: the same as the writing on the love letters she has been receiving for the past thirty years.

'You'd better go.' She says the words so quietly he is not sure he has heard them, or, maybe, hopefully, he imagined them. He is not sure whether to move or not. But she is just staring at him, not blinking.

He stands, tries to think of something to say, but nothing comes to mind. His bottom lip is quivering, and he'd better leave before he loses all control.

Chapter 22

The white paint is runnier than Cosmo expected, and no matter how careful he is it keeps dripping down his brush, over his fingers and onto the floor. He had no idea what he was buying, and the man in the shop in Saros asked him if he wanted oil-based or water-based paint. Thinking the water-based paint would just wash off if it got splashed, he chose oil, not realising until the till rang, and the hardware man told him, that he would need something to get it off the brush and his fingers when he was finished. The smell of the white spirit is not nice, nor for that matter does he like the smell of the paint. But he is breathing in deeply, punishing himself for making such a complete mess of his life.

Another drip, and this one hits his shoe. One of his cuffs is already daubed with paint and wet from a quick soak in white spirit. He would have put an old shirt on if he had known it would be so messy. He tips a little of the white spirit onto the corner of one of his mama's tea towels and dabs at his shoe.

Three days now. Three days since he poured a whole bottle of ouzo down his neck and made the most gigantic mistake of his life.

What was he thinking? He is not good at decision-making when he is sober, so why would he have thought he was any better at it drunk?

'*Gamoto!*' He swears at himself and his behaviour. After carefully resting the paintbrush across the top of the tin, he checks his hands for paint. They are not too bad. He pulls the cooker away from the wall. Spiders run for cover, dusty webs billow in the slight breeze he has created. He will have to clean first. Right now he wishes he had never started the job.

First he runs the broom over the wall, then the drying cloth.

'Good enough,' he comments, and he takes up his paintbrush again.

At least he went to work yesterday and this morning. He thought when he got home on the day Maria told him to leave that he would never go out again, ever. He went to bed and stayed there with his blankets over his head, crying, cursing and sleeping until a cockerel called to him – 'Go-and-get-the-mails'.

He went because he did not want to mess up the only other thing in his life. He went today, too, because he could no longer sleep. He did not loiter on his rounds, or stay to read anyone's mail, and he did not stay to answer anybody's letters for them. Old Lefteris asked what was wrong, seeming concerned, but he could not answer him and hurried off silently, speaking to no one.

After work he bought bread and yoghurt without a word, but he broke his silence at the hardware shop, where he bought paint for the kitchen. He is determined, having bungled things so badly with Maria, to do something positive, to achieve something, even if it is as trivial as getting rid of that sickly pale green.

A particularly thick blob of paint runs down the wall. If it continues its journey it will bury a spider that is motionless in the corner where the wall meets the floor. The brush is balanced across the tin again, and he grabs for the cloth, but too late: the spider is caught. After looking around desperately, he grabs a knife from table and lifts the spider clear of the viscous pool. It struggles to free itself but the paint is too thick. The white covers its legs and body, and it can hardly move. He puts it down on the washing-up sponge and nudges it with the point of the knife. It is alive, at least! He dips the knife end in the white spirit and then hovers the blade over the spider, letting a single drop fall, to wash away the tiniest amount of paint. He repeats the process and the spider lifts one of its legs free.

'Come on, my friend, I would rather have spiders in the house than mosquitoes.'

He lets another drop fall, washing away more of the white goo, which soaks into the sponge. He needs something more delicate than the bread knife. He looks about and spots the jar of toothpicks. These allow the drops to fall directly onto the individual legs of the spider, and the little creepy-crawly begins to respond, lifting one leg, then the other. The tiny creature is almost free of the paint now.

'Do you wash, my friend? How do you clean yourself? This white spirit will do you no good.' Cosmo uses the corner of the drying cloth to drip water, to wash off the white spirit.

Studying the animal this closely, he can make out the hairs on its legs, so small it is a miracle. But they are all clean, every last hair, and there is nothing more he can do. He waits, but the tiny creature does not move.

'Are you beaten, my friend? I know how you feel. Exhausted with life? Join the club. What to do? What can we do? Life is how life is.'

He sighs heavily, his breath on the spider, and then, without warning, his new-found friend runs as fast as it can, along the top of the counter and down the side.

'Ha!' Cosmo erupts in triumph, and with new life he takes up his paintbrush and continues his work until a tap on the door echoes around his otherwise silent kitchen.

He doesn't want to answer. He doesn't want to see anyone.

A face appears at the window, a hand shielding the light, stopping reflections.

'Hey, Cosmo,' Thanasis calls, peering through the glass. 'Is the door open?' A minute later the door latch rattles.

Thanasis is probably the last person on earth he wants to see right now.

'Hey, hey, look at you, Mr Industrious.' Thanasis admires the half-painted room.

Cosmo cannot find any words that he would trust himself to say so he remains silent.

Thanasis sits at the kitchen table like he has a thousand times before, and grins. 'Haven't seen you for a couple of days. I was wondering if everything was all right.'

Cosmo grunts: a relatively positive noise to shut Thanasis up.

'Then I remembered that the last time we spoke I challenged you to a game of *tavli*, so then, of course, I realised why I hadn't seen you. You were just plain scared of the beating I was going to give you.'

He laughs at his own joke and the noise sounds too loud in the small kitchen.

'You got a hangover?' he asks, the silence too much for him.

'No,' Cosmo replies automatically. He will never ever touch the stuff again.

'Ah,' Thanasis says. He is ill at ease. 'So what's your mood all about then? Has something happened...? Ha! Talking of something happening...'

He speaks quickly, not giving Cosmo an opportunity to answer. He needs to say what he needs to say, and quickly, before he falters.

'You will never in a million and one years guess what happened to me the day before yesterday!' Yes, that is as good a way of introducing this topic as any. 'Oh my God, you will never guess! Go on, try.'

Thanasis raises and lowers the pitch of his voice, to make it sound like it was a good thing, something positive.

'Think of the wildest possible thing and you won't even be close ... You want water?'

He stands, hearing the tremor in his voice, and as he takes a glass and runs the tap he can see his hands trembling. Cosmo shakes his head but he does not turn around; he seems reluctant to look his friend in the eye right now.

Sitting again, Thanasis drinks his fill and smacks his lips in satisfaction. 'Let me tell you.' Here goes ...

Cosmo is painting the narrow strip of wall between the corner of the room and the cupboard door. He sighs.

'No! Given up already?' Thanasis continues trying to sound jolly. 'Well, I will tell you who came to visit. Actually came to my home! Are you sure you don't want to guess who? You will never guess, so I will tell you.'

He watches Cosmo dip his brush in the paint and takes a deep breath.

'Maria!'

With a plop the brush slips from Cosmo's hand into the paint bucket and his jaw hangs open.

'Now that's surprised you! It certainly surprised me.' Thanasis feels that if he can keep talking, everything will be all right. Just keep talking.

'Maria?' Cosmo barely whispers his query, picking the brush carefully out of the paint; all the bristles and half the handle are now shiny, wet and white. Cosmo holds the brush between finger and thumb and lets it hang for a moment to allow the bulk of the paint to slide off.

In the short pause Thanasis has allowed, he hears his friend repeat himself.

'Maria?' This time Cosmo sounds more casual. Thanasis's ears have started to ring.

'Yes, Maria from opposite the church!' Right now he needs to explain … 'Well, okay, let me back up a bit, explain something to you. You see, you probably won't remember her from when she was young but she used to be quite a looker and I developed a bit of a crush on her. You know, from afar.'

He watches Cosmo's free hand ball into a fist as his other hand slaps the paint hard onto the wall. This is going to be tough. Keep talking.

'Well, over the years my feelings have waxed and waned, but I have let her know, not too directly, that she was admired. I have written her letters. Ha ha! You have probably delivered them.'

He pretends that he finds this very funny and laughs heartily. It feels like a relief to laugh, but he knows he is just putting off what needs to be said. When he wrote the letters he didn't know Maria could not read. He had no idea, and the horror of this discovery, along with the knowledge of the fact that Cosmo has had to read his love letters to her over the years, is no joke! It is totally embarrassing. Right now he must not think of himself but of Cosmo – and Maria.

Cosmo is showing nothing outwardly, he just paints – slap, slap. Keep talking, Thanasis tells himself. If he stops now his own cowardice may stop him forever.

'Well, in all the years I sent them, she never answered my letters, which is not surprising as I never signed them. You see, I was never really sure.'

It seemed all right at the time, but now, saying it out loud, it's clear it was a selfish game to have played. 'I mean, I did have feelings for her and I kind of liked the idea of a bit of a romance in my life, but the reality? So I kept it, you know, sort of dreamy. She could dream of who this mysterious lover was and I could have a little dream too. No harm.'

He stands, his chair scraping harshly across the floor. Cosmo still hasn't turned around. Thanasis's glass catches the light and sparkles as he takes it to the sink, turning on the tap and listening to the familiar groan of the pipes, before the water rushes out.

Cosmo is concentrating on getting a straight edge with the white paint next to the cupboard, but his hand is shaking and he cannot control the brush.

'Anyway,' Thanasis continues. He thinks he catches Cosmo looking down and under his own raised arm, at him. He looks away to his own calloused hands as he toys with his glass, making the bottom rock around on the table, the water trying to find its level up the side of the glass.

'I don't know how, but she found out it was me.' He feels like he has lost momentum and the words no longer sound jolly, but forced and dry instead. 'Now, I have always thought of Maria as having grown to be a bit of a bitter woman, perhaps, over the years, but still mild and meek. I never reckoned on her being feisty.' His voice sounds positively sad.

Cosmo's tension is filling the room; Thanasis could cut it with a knife. He would like to open the window or the door, let some new air in – even better, go outside himself. He does neither of these things but instead continues determinedly.

'So I am out the back of the house, and I hear someone shifting the gate and naturally I assume it is you, so I call out, "*Ela* Cosmo", but you don't reply. So I stop fixing the trough, or whatever I was doing, and wait to see who appears. You could have knocked me down with a feather. It was Maria! What's more, I immediately know it is not a normal sort of house call' – Cosmo stops painting, his brush paused – 'because she still has her apron on!' The paint in the corner where Cosmo is working is drying and dragging, he has been over it so many times now.

'"Explain yourself," she demands, just like that, as if I have done something wrong,' Thanasis continues, trying to inject some humour into his voice.

Cosmo turns the corner to the last, small section of wall, his brush moving so slowly. Thanasis can tell that he does not want to finish because then he will be forced to turn and face his friend. He pushes on, trying to make the situation easier for both of them.

'"Explain what?" I ask, all innocent, like. Well, how was I to know what she meant? But in my heart I sort of knew it must be something to do with the letters. After all, we have no other connection.'

'Now, I want to try and explain this to you so you get a full picture of this woman, Cosmo. I feel I owe you that.'

What he has done has been so selfish. Why did he not see it this way all these years? His cheeks are hot and his eyes mist over. But he must warn his friend too – Maria is not all sweetness and light, it is important that he knows that too.

Cosmo stops painting, but he remains with his back to his friend.

Thanasis is transported by his own words back to the events of that day.

She stood there with her hands on her hips, her face stern and those beautiful eyes of hers looking so hurt. The fig tree behind her, dark within its branches, made her stand out in her sunlit patch.

'You have no idea what you have done,' she said. He was about to protest when she took the bundle of envelopes from the pocket of her apron. In that second, blood rushed to his ears, setting them ringing; his cheeks were on fire and one leg began to tremble. Adrenaline shot through his chest, and in his panic his throat seemed to tighten. Stupidly, or so he thought afterwards, his first response was concern, in case she wanted to take him up on his offer of love, make something of it. And in that moment he asked himself if he would really want that – if he was ready?

He can remember the smell of the donkeys behind him at that point and, as if for the first time, seeing his own yard as others might see it – bare of any sense of civilisation, with compacted earth and crates for seats, not even a chair. Bags of rubbish waiting to be taken to the bins, and bags of manure stacked in one corner. He tried to search his heart and, sure enough, there was a big open cavity of loneliness and just a little fear of growing any older alone. So he smiled and, foolishly, put out his hands to implore her.

'Maria, you have seen how long I have had a candle burning for you,' he said.

At first she did not respond and he wondered if he should retract it or say it again, but then she took a step closer and he did not know if she was going to kiss him or slap him. He noticed he felt scared of either possibility.

'You never had the courage or the human decency to even sign your name,' she said, and her words cut him, because he knew it was the truth. She didn't exactly growl these words, but even if she had she could not have sounded more threatening. But in his fear and – he could admit to himself afterwards – his arrogance, he did wonder at the time if this was her way of courtship, establishing who was boss, so to speak.

'A little intrigue,' he answered gaily, covering his uncertainty, his shame, and, to be honest, his fear. There was menace in the woman. But there was no stopping her – it was as if the spring rains had come and she was making up for all her years of silence.

'Well, your little "intrigue" has had consequences and now you will put it right,' she said. It was not a question and he did not feel like he could argue. She looked around, and when she saw that there was no chair or bench, she pointed at an orange crate and said 'Sit,' as if he were a dog. She had a commanding manner, and he did as he was bid. She remained standing.

'You will go to Cosmo,' she began – and that was when he became very confused and opened his mouth to speak, but she hissed at him to be quiet. He had no idea what Cosmo had to do with this. Surely it was just him writing letters to her, and she was – what? Cross, insulted? Adding Cosmo to the mix was just plain confusing.

'You will go to Cosmo,' she said, 'and you will explain what you have done, and you will apologise to him for your selfish, self-serving little game.'

He heard her words and they served to mystify him but also, at that point, it was as if she had pushed just a little too hard, and anger stirred within him. He had not been spoken to like that since his yiayia died, crazy in her old age and no longer aware of who he was. So he stood; it was a reflex. But she locked her eyes on him and gave him such a withering look that his knees gave way and he sat again, meekly. In all the years he had written to her, he had no idea that this was the type of woman she really was. But he was about to get to know her even better because when Maria spoke again it was like an explosion.

'What did you think I would think of your anonymous love letters?' She spat the words out, but she was not expecting any sort of answer because she continued without pausing to let him speak.

'At first I was confused,' she said. 'I thought it was someone being unkind, making a joke out of the fact I had been left high and dry.' And it was only then that he vaguely recalled she had been jilted, and he cringed at his own insensitivity. But there was no space for apologies.

'It hurt,' she continued. 'It hurt deeply and I was too embarrassed to go out of my own front door because I didn't know who was playing this cruel joke. Was it just one person or the whole village? I became afraid to go out because I thought the world was laughing at me, and you did that, Thanasi. You!'

He felt his lips curl in self-admonition as he began to realise that his silly little letters were the reason beautiful Maria had shied away from the world. He muttered something like *'Thée mou'*, hoping his god would step in and redeem him as she continued.

'The letters kept coming, one every six months, and I began to realise that this was not someone being cruel, but someone who maybe did harbour feelings for me.' She had been speaking to the open air as she said all this, but now she glared at him.

'I am not blind, Thanasi. I saw the way Cosmo looked at me and so I began to wonder if they were from him, and it drove a wedge between us. I thought he wasn't brave enough to confess, and that he disguised his handwriting so that I wouldn't know. And he, no doubt, was embarrassed by having to read someone else's love letters.'

And in that moment, he realised that she could not read, and the enormity of what he had done to his friend covered him like the heavy clouds of a storm. His heart sank and he wondered if there would ever be a way out.

'I swear, I did not know that you could not read,' he started. 'It never occurred to me. Nor for one second did I ever think that Cosmo would be reading those letters to you, and I swear on my mama's grave, I swear to God' - and he crossed himself for added sincerity - 'I did not think for a second that Cosmo ever harboured any feelings of affection for you. I really didn't.'

He didn't think she believed him but his thoughts were now for Cosmo and he found himself struggling in an unfamiliar place, which, if he had to label it, he would call regret.

He only half heard her as she talked on, comparing his writing with some of Cosmo's writing – a letter he had written for her, or something. As she talked, it sank in that Cosmo held her in high regard, and he began to think of a hundred and one tiny events that pointed to this in the past, signs he had ignored, or even, to his shame, made a joke of. Like the time Cosmo stood for her to pass in church and, once she was seated, handed her his prayer book. Thanasis himself had only been there because it was Petta's wedding, and he had thought Cosmo was teasing her with this behaviour.

Another time, he caught Cosmo holding the lid of the bin for Maria to put her rubbish in, the cats all around her ankles. He had not taken that seriously. But now, the more he brought to mind such events, the more he realised that it was not in Cosmo's nature to tease in that way and that his actions towards others were motivated by respect. He was not sure what hit him harder: the surprise, or the horror of what he had done.

'What are you saying about Cosmo?' he asked, in an attempt to deflect her attention from himself to his friend. 'Do you mean that you, and Cosmo, the two of you …?'

He did not laugh – he could have sworn he did not laugh. He might have smiled, not in fun, but because he was pleased. Pleased to have Maria's focus off him, and because Maria was not calling him out on the love he could not provide, and not least at the thought that Cosmo and Maria might have a stab at a little mortal happiness. Yes, he was pleased.

'You laugh!' Maria's voice was so loud he could have sworn the leaves on his orange trees rattled and the donkeys turned their ears backward. 'You write of your love and your longing, of watching me from afar and considering my beauty, of your esteem for my elegant conduct over my parents' death!'

She pulled a letter from the pile and held it in front of her as if quoting from it. 'You go on about your admiration of my kindness to animals, but what good are all those wild, flourishing words to a woman? Cosmo has been by my side through the rejection by my fiancé, he gave me space when I needed to heal, and he came back when I needed his companionship again. He has been there for me, through everything, for the last thirty years and in all that time he asked nothing for himself. He has listened to me talk, laugh, cry and moan. He comforted me when first my baba and then my mama died, and he has kept me company every few days ever since, whether he had the excuse of a letter to deliver or not. He has continued to be my friend even when the village has come to view me as a bitter, reclusive old woman. Yes, I am aware of what they say.'

Her eyes flashed, defying him to deny this.

'And I am aware it does Cosmo no good at all to be seen as my ally, but he is there for me anyway. There have been no pretty words or false promises, only actions that prove his devotion. And I have waited, Thanasi, I have waited these thirty years to find out who this letter writer was that was stopping Cosmo declaring himself. And do you know why it stopped him? Do you?'

Her finger jabbed at him – her nail sharpened to a point, he could have sworn. 'Because in his self-effacing way, he believes the letter writer has first claim on me, because the letter writer announced his love first.'

She pauses as if in triumph. 'That' – she pauses again – 'is how uncomplicated his mind is, and that' – another pause – 'is how pure his thoughts are.'

It was at this point that she took off the string that held the bundle of his love letters together and she threw them, envelopes and all, in his face. Not on the floor, or vaguely in his direction, but actually in his face. A feisty woman.

After he got over the shock of the corners digging into his cheek and one nearly taking his eye out, he murmured a lot of words to explain how he had meant no harm, that it was a bit of fun, that it was meant to make her feel good to have a secret admirer. But he could hear the hollowness of his own selfish words as they left his lips, and it did not surprise him at all when she sucked her teeth at him and looked down that straight nose of hers as if he was nothing. Her derision reflected how he felt about himself at that moment.

But even then she was not finished, and he began to despair.

'Your affection for me was from your own imagination,' she hissed, her face inches from his. 'Your letters served your own purpose – they offered me nothing.'

And then came the crushing blow he had been expecting.

'You will go to Cosmo and you will tell him what you have done and tell him that you retract any claim he thinks you might have on me, and you will encourage him to confess his feelings to me. You will urge him to confess, you hear me, because neither I nor he is getting any younger.'

And in the silence that followed this torrent of words, it hit him with a horrifying sense of reality that he must do all the things Maria had said, to make things right.

The silence in the kitchen is deafening as Thanasis finally stops talking. The paint has dripped down the brush, over Cosmo's hand and wrist, and off the end of his elbow onto his already-tainted shoe as he stares open-mouthed at his friend. Thanasis stares back, looking into one of his eyes and then the other, trying to read his friend's expression. His brow keeps furrowing into the deep crease between his eyes. His eyebrows do not know whether to lift or fall. Cosmo has no idea if seconds or minutes pass, and he is not sure if the ground beneath his feet is moving, or if the room is spinning.

Thanasis colours red and coughs. He seems to have realised something.

'I'll tell you one thing, my friend.'

His tone is falsely jolly as he stands.

'That is one bullet that I am glad I dodged. Wow! That is one feisty wench.' He is talking too fast. 'Whoever ends up with her, I wish them well, I really do, but it will take quite a man to tackle that one, and rest assured, Cosmo, my dear friend, that man is not me. No, that is not me for sure. It is a better man than me who takes that one on! Now, where are we? Oh Lord,' he says, looking up at the cuckoo clock, its hands still motionless. 'Is that the time? I must go to feed the donkeys.'

And he is out of the door and round past the window before Cosmo can fully take in what has just happened.

He is still standing there when there is a second tap on the door. Thinking it is Thanasis come back, he is both reluctant to answer and curious too. Surely there can be no more to say? In fact, he has not completely processed what has been said so far. He is still unravelling it; his mouth keeps flickering into a smile, but he needs to replay some of the words Thanasis said over in his head to make sure what just happened really took place.

'Was he saying what I think he was saying?' he mutters to himself, and he opens the door, deciding to ask Thanasis to speak in plainer words, so he can take it in.

'Cosmo?' the stranger asks.

'Er.' He is not sure he wants to commit himself.

'Thanasis the donkey breeder told me you had early oranges to sell.'

The man smiles and puts out his hand to shake, and Cosmo is lifted out of his thoughts to focus on the need to sell his harvest.

Chapter 23

The next morning, Cosmo's head is still spinning. Despite his efforts to find Thanasis, he has not managed to see him again. At one point, the situation seemed desperate and he even drove from one bar to the next in Saros, searching for signs of his friend. He needed confirmation of what he thought had been said.

The more he thinks about it, the less he dares trust his own interpretation, but Thanasis has gone to ground and Cosmo's thoughts have continued to make him dizzy through each hour that passes. In any given moment, he might feel confident that what he believed, hoped, could be possible is in fact true. But as soon as he has this thought, his brain tells him not to talk such nonsense and he forces himself to dismiss the possibility as ridiculous once more.

Back and forth he has gone. Now, after a brief, restless sleep, Cosmo still needs to speak to Thanasis, to put himself out of this misery of hoping and get his friend to confirm what he said.

'Or deny it.' Cosmo lets the wind take his words as he speeds toward the village with the morning's mail.

There is not much of it today, and he partially sorted through it at the depot. He stacked all of Sakis's letters together, and a few others for the same street, and that accounted for all but a handful of the post, which he can easily sort as he makes his way from cottage to cottage.

But first to drop off Sakis's letters. As usual, the musician can be heard around the back of his cottage, the beautiful, melodic strumming of his guitar drifting off and becoming muffled in the orange grove at the back of his house. Cosmo lingers for a few moments. The sound seems to soothe his soul, and when Sakis starts to sing Cosmo cannot move.

'I didn't set my alarm last night … I woke up this morning with the new sun gently warming …'

The breeze snatches the next few words and notes away with it, but then they return:

'Outside I listened to the birds
They didn't chastise me for
my ignoring them for so long
They were happy to have my ears back
to listen to their song
I was happy to listen
I was lost without thought
A deeper connection that leaves me vacant to not think
and just be

for this moment amongst the orange trees.'

Then the guitar takes over again and Cosmo pushes the letters through the door so he can free up his hand to wipe a tear from his eye.

He used to be like that, with nothing on his mind, waking up with the sun, listening to the birds, just being, and in those pleasant days people called him lazy, slow and simple. Well, they don't call him lazy or slow or simple any more. They use expressions like 'hard-working' and 'blossoming', whatever that is supposed to mean!

These new labels give him no pleasure. The hard work and the complexity of his life nowadays is not something that has enriched his world. It steals his time and makes his head spin until the days pass in a blur, and he finds he has not felt any of them. When did he last take the time to listen to a bird?

He delivers other letters down the street. His bike is misfiring again. One day it will give up, cough and die and he will have to learn how to fix it because he cannot afford to take it to a garage – or can he? Maybe that was another myth of his mama's, like the expense of clothes. She might have made his life simpler by forever treating him as if he was five, but she also made him more fearful of what might happen.

But she has been dead ten months now. He is no longer afraid of what might happen.

What happens, happens – there is no cure and no putting it off. The trick is just to roll with the waves. But he could get back to things being simpler. Sell the orchard, and stop reading and writing people's letters. Or maybe give up the post office job and concentrate on the oranges after all. That would be the simplest: nothing but oranges, which do not talk back or ask him to write letters.

A flying bug crosses his path, bouncing off his chest. He looks down at himself. There is paint on his new shirt, the cuff is torn, and his shoes are smeared with a sheen of white spirit. He is not good at looking after himself.

There are only two letters left. The top one is for Marina at the corner shop. He gives this to Theo, who is just going in the door there – and the last …

'Too cruel,' he whispers at his fate as he sees that it is addressed to Maria. He will not knock, just slip it under her door. If he is going to find any peace over this whole business he needs to talk to Thanasis first before he sees Maria … If he ever sees her again, that is, and at the moment it is the last thing he wants. He is just so exhausted by it all.

He stops his bike on the corner that leads down to his house, pushes it back onto its stand and, with his head bent, goes to push Maria's letter under the door. The thin white envelope, with its typed address, slides underneath easily and quietly and he has begun to walk away when the door slightly opens, and he freezes, caught out.

'Come in.'

She speaks through the crack. He cannot tell if it is a request or a command. He rubs his forehead.

'Please,' she adds, which makes him look towards her, but she is gone, leaving the door ajar.

He is not sure he can face this now. The emotions that have been sweeping through him since the night he wrote the letter have drained him of all emotion. He is like a grape still hanging from the vine in December, shrivelled and dry. He is cleared out, unreachable, and there is no fight left in him.

Reluctant feet scuff his shoes over the threshold, through Maria's door and into the kitchen, which is filled with the smell of freshly baked biscuits. Two coffee cups sit ready at the table and the water in the *briki* is boiling.

She makes the first coffee in silence and Cosmo sits heavily at the table, head bowed, fingers interlocked in front of him; his satchel is still over his shoulder, across his chest, hitching his winter jacket up into an uncomfortable mess under his armpit, but he does not care.

'There you are.' She puts the first coffee in front of him. It takes a few minutes for the grounds to settle and in that time she has made her own. She sits beside him, picks up a biscuit and breaks it in two, handing him half. It is such a familiar action that, despite himself, he looks up at her face. She is smiling; her face is soft, the harshness gone and with it many of the years.

He nibbles on the biscuit.

'Is it good?'

'Your biscuits have always been good,' he says cautiously.

'I have listened to what you have said about them over the years and used it to improve them to your taste.'

She dips her own biscuit in her coffee, holds it there, just for a second, and then transfers it to her mouth, first sucking then crunching.

'Oh.' Cosmo can think of nothing more to say in reply but she is looking at him expectantly. 'I am tired, Maria,' he says.

'It is too much for a man,' she replies.

He frowns.

'To go to work, to keep a farm, keep a house, look after himself, cook, wash clothes, sweep floors, go shopping. Too much.' She shakes her head.

Cosmo's frown deepens. He neither cooks, nor shops, nor washes his clothes. He looks at his hand and sees his torn sleeve, the remains of the paint, and he understands what she is saying.

'Yes,' he says.

'It's funny, isn't it?'

Her voice lightens and she takes another biscuit, breaks it in two and gives him half. He has not finished his first half yet, but he takes the second anyway.

'All day I keep house, sweep floors, cook, bake and mend but there is no one to appreciate what I do. Here we are, just a few steps away from each other, and you work all day and have no one to take these chores off your shoulders.'

For a moment he wonders if she is asking for a job, but then she takes out the letter he wrote when he was drunk. With his elbows on the table and his fingers interlocked, he knocks his thumbs against his forehead and screws up his eyes at the sight of it. He is going to refuse to deal with this today. He just doesn't have the energy for it if she is going to tell him off as she did Thanasis. At least he, Cosmo, signed his name.

'Your letter finished with a question,' she says, smoothing the missive on the table.

He closes his eyes even tighter.

'The answer is yes.'

He has forgotten the question. Well, he hasn't, but he must have, because the answer to what he thinks he asked would not be 'yes', would it? He opens one eye, just a fraction, to see where she is, to see if she is looking at him, but her eyes are fixed on the paper, her finger tracing the lines of text.

'I have been learning all these years, Cosmo. Very slowly, but I have been learning. I can make out the letters and these here say "Will you marry me?". And my answer is yes.'

'What?'

'Yes.'

He stares.

'You mean …'

'Yes.'

'Because you pity me?'

'No.'

'Because …'

She puts her hand on his and it shuts him up.

'Because your heart is the purest of any I know, and the kindest, and the most sincere.' Maria's next action is one Cosmo has dreamt about, but never imagined would really happen. She leans over the table and kisses him full on the mouth.

The softness of her lips is beyond what he imagined, the give of the muscles around her mouth more bewitching than he could ever have expected, but, almost immediately, it is something other than the texture of the kiss that keeps his focus: instead, he is aware of her yielding to him. It is unspoken, but he knows it is happening, as if she has no will of her own; then it changes again, and he can sense her urgency, her insistence.

They are talking without words and he has never had such a wonderful, expansive conversation. He is being lifted up and up, they have left the ground and they are flying together, she is allowing him to lead, and yet she is showing him the way. Where he ends and she begins is no longer clear and for the first time in his life all his awkwardness is gone, all his insecurities have melted away and he feels complete.

Finally, she pulls away, but he doesn't want her to go. He seeks her lips with his and they meet again, but the two of them have grounded now and she kisses him again and again, shorter and shorter pecks until at last they draw apart a little; she looks at him directly and he sees her love for him in her eyes, sucking him in and under until he would drown, and be happy to, were it not for the expansion in his chest keeping him afloat. The adrenaline in his limbs tells him he could run a thousand miles, lift a building from its foundations or turn Maria from a mortal to a goddess. His hand shoots up to the back of her head, his fingers in her slightly greying hair, and he pulls her back to him, eager to join with the other half of his soul again.

Their coffee goes cold, as do the freshly baked biscuits, and the official letter he is there to deliver remains unopened on the table for the next hour. They manage a small amount of talk between kisses. Their bodies demand that they become closer, and Cosmo lifts her slight weight so she is sitting on his knee; there they remain as they sort through all the misunderstandings and complications of the years gone by. They regret and forget them in the moment and discover that the outcome could never have been anything other than this: their lives were always heading toward this predestined conclusion. They straighten the path that has been and clear the route for the future.

When they finally come up for air and remember the world around them, Maria makes fresh coffee and taps the letter that Cosmo is here to deliver.

'I think you will find that this is for you,' she says, and she puts the water on to boil.

He tears it open and reads the heading. 'It is from Babis the lawyer.'

'Yes,' she says.

'It is your will. I should not be reading this. Get Babis to read it for you.'

'Please read it, I want to check it is as I asked.'

'It says that you will leave everything … to me!'

She smiles. 'Of course, who else? I have no intention of outlasting you. I have spent enough time alone.'

A mischievous smile kindles her eyes as she puts his coffee down beside him; then, from under a side table, she lifts a wooden box, takes from it a needle and thread and sits down again and, taking hold of his sleeve, starts to repair the tear in stitches so tiny he can hardly see them.

Chapter 24

Thanasis has won for the fourth time.

'When you meet your master it is better just to accept it,' he says, taunting. He closes the *tavli* box and hails Theo for an ouzo.

'You want one or are you still not drinking?'

'Definitely not drinking.' Cosmo laughs.

'You know, I think you are looking at this all wrong. If it hadn't been for the drink, you would never have written the letter, never posted it. Maria would never have come round to me and she would not have forced your hand. So really, it is because you were drunk that you got the girl!'

He turns his head towards the counter. 'Two ouzos, Theo!' he calls.

'One,' Cosmo corrects.

Theo brings two glasses and fills one. Thanasis points to the second but Cosmo turns it upside down. Theo chuckles and leaves, taking the bottle with him.

'Ah, give it time and you will be in here like the rest of them, getting out of the house and licking their wounds. Have you set a date yet?' Thanasis asks.

'The papas says he can marry us a week next Saturday, but Maria wants it to be a small affair, so keep that to yourself until I know how she wants to play it.' Cosmo grins from ear to ear.

'You see, already she is calling the shots,' Thanasis teases.

Cosmo thrills at these words. It is going to be wonderful; in fact, it already is wonderful, with Maria taking over all the decision-making in his life. She cooks and shops, the house is clean, and she loves the white walls in the kitchen. So far she has not chosen which house they will live in, but she has decided that whichever it is they will rent out the other to make their lives a little more comfortable.

He could not wish for more, except perhaps to share her bed. But that will be fulfilled in due course, when they are married. Although, if he is honest with himself, as each day passes, he feels a certain amount of apprehension over this. But then he comforts himself that she will too. They are both in the same boat.

'Yeia sou, Cosmo.' A farmer from the next village enters and comes straight up to him and shakes his hand.

'I hear you got the reward. You want an ouzo?' He raises a finger to Theo.

'No, thanks. Yes, I got the reward. Never thought such things were real, but I guess I saved a lot of people's oranges.'

'You did indeed.' The farmer pats him heartily on his shoulder and wanders off to find a table.

'Have they actually given you the cash yet?' Thanasis asks.

'Got it and spent it.'

'What, all of it?'

'It wasn't that much. I got the fan fixed. It needed a whole new motor after all. The back fence is replaced and Maria is keeping some back in case we need new furniture.'

'She has your purse strings already!'

Thanasis laughs. Both his laughter and his words are quiet, without malice, but a brief cloud does pass across his eyes, and Cosmo wonders if Thanasis might be feeling just a touch of jealousy.

'Babis wanted to hold on to it for me,' Cosmo says.

'Ha!' Thanasis explodes.

'Exactly! He kept making all these excuses, and I couldn't get hold of it. But Maria paid him a visit, and half an hour later, not only was the reward transferred to my bank account but probate was complete at no further cost either, just like that!'

Thanasis whistles through his teeth.

'So you got it all, eh, my friend? The girl, the reward …'

The farmer from the next village is leaving already and he nods at Cosmo.

'And the respect of the village,' Thanasis adds.

'Oh,' Cosmo says. 'Talking of the respect of the village' – Cosmo adopts a slightly mocking tone to indicate he does not accept this accolade – 'here, happy name day.'

From his pocket, he pulls the card he had signed by everyone.

'What's this?' Thanasis asks.

'It's a card – you know, like they give for birthdays and celebrations and things.' Cosmo bites his bottom lip, not sure how Thanasis will receive his offering.

Thanasis tears it open and reads down the list of names, Cosmo's and Maria's at the bottom.

'Oh – that is really nice.' There is a break in Thanasis's voice and Cosmo can tell the thoughtfulness has touched him.

After a few minutes, in which Thanasis studies the card, Cosmo says, 'Right, I need to get going.'

'Now? It's a bit early, isn't it?' Thanasis knocks back his half-drunk glass of ouzo.

'Oh, but Maria is baking some biscuits,' Cosmo says. 'A new recipe.'

'Ah, there is a lucky man, who can be satisfied with a plate of warm biscuits!' Thanasis stands to leave too.

'Says the man who cannot wait to get back to his donkeys,' Cosmo chuckles.

They stand on the top step of the *kafenio*, side by side, the sun slanting across the square at an angle, softening the kiosk and the fountain and the palm tree and blurring the shadows. The whitewashed cottages around them glow a soft pink, the terracotta tiles a warm red.

'Ah, but I didn't tell you, did I?'

'What?' Cosmo rocks contentedly onto his heels and back, hands in pockets.

'I had Coco checked out after the police brought her back. Guess what? She's going to have a foal.'

'Ha!' Cosmo laughs. 'It goes to show that it is never too late for any of us.'

<<##>>

Good reviews are important to a novel's success and will help others find *A Self Effacing Man*. If you enjoyed it, please be kind and leave a review wherever you purchased the book.

I'm always delighted to receive email from readers, and I welcome new friends on Facebook.

Facebook:
> https://www.facebook.com/authorsaraalexi

Email: saraalexi@me.com

Happy reading,

Sara Alexi

Also by Sara Alexi

The Illegal Gardener
Black Butterflies
The Explosive Nature of Friendship
The Gypsy's Dream
The Art of Becoming Homeless
In the Shade of the Monkey Puzzle Tree
A Handful of Pebbles
The Unquiet Mind
Watching the Wind Blow
The Reluctant Baker
The English Lesson
The Priest's Well
A Song Amongst the Orange Trees
The Stolen Book
The Rush Cutter's Legacy
Saving Septic Cyril : The Illegal Gardener Part II
Being Enough
A Stranger in the Village

PUBLISHED BY:

Oneiro Press

A Self Effacing Man
Book Nineteen of the Greek Village Collection

Copyright © 2016 by Sara Alexi

This is a work of fiction. All of the characters, organisations, and events portrayed in this novel are either products of the author's imagination or are used fictitiously.

Printed in Great Britain
by Amazon